# Anjum's EAT RIGHT FOR YOUR BODY TYPE

## THE SUPER-HEALTHY DETOX DIET INSPIRED BY AYURVEDA

### ANJUM ANAND

Photography by Lisa Linder

Da Capo
LIFE LONG

To my mother, who urges me to keep my life simple,
and to my father, who inspires me to live it to the fullest.

Text © 2010 by Anjum Anand
Photographs © 2010 Lisa Linder
Design and layout © 2010 Quadrille
Publishing Ltd

Cataloging-in-Publication data for this book is
available from the Library of Congress.
First Da Capo Press edition 2011
ISBN 978-0-7382-1494-8

First published by Quadrille Publishing Ltd.
Published by Da Capo Press
A Member of the Perseus Books Group
www.dacapopress.com

Note: This book is intended only as an
informative guide for those wishing to know
more about health issues. In no way is this
book intended to replace, countermand, or
conflict with the advice given to you by your
own physician. The ultimate decision
concerning care should be made between you
and your doctor. We strongly recommend you
follow his or her advice. Information in this
book is general and is offered with no
guarantees on the part of the authors or Da
Capo Press. The authors and publisher
disclaim all liability in connection with the use
of this book.

Da Capo Press books are available at special
discounts for bulk purchases in the U.S. by
corporations, institutions, and other
organizations. For more information, please
contact the Special Markets Department at
the Perseus Books Group, 2300 Chestnut
Street, Suite 200, Philadelphia, PA, 19103, or
call (800) 810-4145, ext. 5000, or e-mail
special.markets@perseusbooks.com.

# CONTENTS

# Introduction

I stumbled onto Ayurveda accidentally. Although part of my Indian heritage, it was not something we were taught or ever talked about. But it was there to be seen in my mother's cooking, in her attitude, and in her advice: "don't eat this if you have a cold," "you aren't feeling well, I'll make you some …," or "have a spoon of … to settle your stomach." It was there throughout my childhood so I must have known, on a subconscious level, that food and health were closely linked, but it didn't make it to the front of my consciousness until much later.

Ayurveda is one of the oldest medical systems on Earth and its principles are still being passed down, orally, from one generation to the next. I discovered Ayurveda properly around nine years ago. I started having a few health issues that I was unable to shake off. My digestion was slow and I was getting bloated every day, I was easily tired and very moody. In addition, I was gaining weight despite being on the same low-fat diet that helped me lose all my excess weight (see page 42) and was exercising regularly. I consulted doctors and met nutritionists, but no one could offer an explanation or solution to any of my problems, simply blaming stress I did not have.

But I wasn't getting better and needed to find answers. My frustration at the situation led me to search further afield and one such tangent brought me to Ayurveda. I met a fantastic Ayurvedic doctor who listened patiently as I went through my issues and history. He did his own examination (an Ayurvedic doctor assesses your health by feeling your pulse with three fingers as well as other things). He explained that my body was imbalanced, that years of yo-yo dieting followed by my own healthy but intensive diet and my need to be constantly active all led to a vata-imbalance and a weakened digestive system.

The doctor gave me some herbal medicines and lots of advice on how to address the balance through diet and lifestyle. It worked and the symptoms started to subside. Intrigued, I started reading books on Ayurveda and I now see the body and health in a completely different way and understand better how to keep myself healthy.

This book introduces Ayurveda in a manner that is simple enough for us to incorporate into a busy twenty-first century life. It explains how and why we are all different and how to eat and live for optimum health. I am forever amazed at the level of knowledge that existed 5,000 years ago and the principles of Ayurveda are as relevant today as they were then, as the human body has evolved little since. There is a Sanskrit word, *kratu*, which translates as "intelligent action"; Ayurveda gives us all the information we need to practice intelligent action in our lives. Our weight, health, and happiness are all in our own hands.

# Origins of Ayurveda

Ayurveda means "science" or "knowledge of life" and is thought to be over 5,000 years old, although the exact date and its origins are shrouded in ancient history and myth.

Popular folklore says that 5,000 years ago, India's greatest sages and "truth seers" went to the Himalayas to meditate on the secrets of health and longevity. While in deep meditation, they are said to have observed the rhythms of the universe and the flows of energy that make up and connect everything in nature. This insight formed the basis of Ayurveda. It was refined and passed down, orally, for thousands of years before being committed to text around 1,000 BC.

This medicine flourished in India for thousands of years before being outlawed by the British when they colonized India. However, it remained the first port of call for the masses outside of the cities so never went away.

## What is Ayurveda?

Ayurveda has two aspects or sides, the preventative side and the curative side. The preventative side guides us on how to avoid illness with the right diet and lifestyle, meditation and yoga. The curative side consists of eight branches of medicine—internal medicine; surgery; pediatrics; psychiatry; treatment of eyes, ears, nose, throat, and head; toxicology; rejuvenation; aphrodisiacs. It is said that Ayurveda influenced early health care around the globe, and many traditional Eastern medical systems are thought to have their roots in Ayurveda.

## How it works

According to the ancient seers, everything in the world is simply a constant play of dynamic forces and energies. Try to imagine different energies as colored smoke, and we would have multiple ribbons of color coming into and leaving the body. It is these energies that connect us so firmly to nature, as everything in nature is made up from these energies (see page 6) and understanding how they flow and work is the key to health. Ayurveda breaks this concept down into bite-sized, digestible pieces which encompass diet, lifestyle, actions, and attitude. It believes everything we need to be healthy is all around us and empowers us to be our own healers.

Ayurveda is a holistic science that believes in the unity of mind, body, and soul, so being ill in one area can affect you in another. As a very general example, we know that continual stress (mind) can cause an ulcer (body); if the ulcers persist and become debilitating, this can affect you on a deeper level, causing despair or depression (soul).

Our bodies innately demand good health and are self-regulating, so managing stress can alleviate all three problems. Ayurveda endeavors to stop us from becoming ill in the first instance, but if you do become unwell, Ayurveda looks for the root of the problem and addresses this issue, rather than the symptoms.

"You don't need medicine when your diet is right and it is not medicine you need if your diet is wrong." old Indian proverb

# The Five Elements

Ayurveda believes that everything in the universe is made up of five elements: ether, air, fire, water, and earth. These elements are energies; finer than molecules and particles, together they are the building blocks of all we see— trees, plants, animals, humans, and even the seasons.

These energies differ from one another only by their density and vibration. The subtlest element is ether, which condenses to become air. As air moves, it causes friction which causes heat or fire. This fire produces moisture which condenses to become water, which ultimately condenses to become earth, the densest element.

The earth element represents all visible solid matter and imparts stability, permanence, and rigidity. In our bodies this translates to our tissues, bones, teeth, and cell structure. Water can be seen in anything with moisture. A large part of our body is water; our blood and the fluids inside and around each cell.

Fire shows itself in anything that is hot, acidic, or combusting. In the body it is represented by the digestive enzymes and body temperature. Air is the wind, it is mobile and dynamic, and in the body it governs all movements and actions, internal and external. Ether is the space in which everything happens.

To maintain health, we need to be able to identify these elemental energies but, as they are invisible, we look instead to their inherent qualities. Each element has a handful of defining qualities, obvious ones being "heat" for fire, "dry" for air, "moist" for water, and "stable" for earth, but there are many more (see Qualities of the Doshas, page 12). These qualities are constant and can be perceived in ourselves, our food, environment, and activities, and are the telltale footprints of the elements.

# The Doshas

In the body, the five elements (air, ether, fire, water, and earth) become biological elements and are grouped into three energies known as doshas.

 The **Vata** dosha is made of air and ether

 The **Pitta** dosha is made of fire and a little water

 The **Kapha** dosha is made of earth and water

Our body is made up of all three doshas and together they are responsible for everything that happens within our bodies. However, like the individuality of a snowflake, we are all made up of the same elements but we are not all the same. This is because the doshas are rarely present in equal proportions; we are born with our own unique ratio of the doshas. This distinct combination makes us who we are and gives us our natural constitution, or prakruti. Your prakruti is like your DNA and comes from your parents' own prakruti and your mother's lifestyle and diet when pregnant. It determines what we look like, our temperament, our character, how we sleep, and how we approach and deal with situations.

As it is rare for us to have equal amounts of all three doshas, one or two will dominate. This dominant dosha becomes known as your own dosha and is there to remind you which element is naturally high in your body and therefore which element to be particularly careful of. If you have more pitta in your body, you will be a pitta dosha or pitta mind/body type, so this is the element you need to monitor in your diet and actions. So you might avoid spending too much time in the sun or eating hot, spicy meals. Most of us have two dominant doshas, for example you could be vata/kapha or pitta/kapha (the most dominant dosha goes first). You can also have all three doshas balanced and be tridoshic, but it is rare.

# Which Dosha Are You?

This questionnaire will help you clarify which doshas dominate in your body. We have all three doshas within us so you will find yourself ticking boxes in all three columns, but ultimately one or two will dominate.

To find out what your natural (birth) constitution (prakruti) is, answer the questions so they reflect you in your most natural state. I answer them looking back at how I was when I was young, when outside pressures did not influence my natural habits and patterns. Then answer the questions again according to who you are now. This will show any current imbalance. Always tackle this imbalance first when choosing food. Use a pencil so that you can keep coming back to it to check your current state.

| | VATA | ✔ | PITTA | ✔ | KAPHA | ✔ |
|---|---|---|---|---|---|---|
| **Frame** | Tall or short with little body fat and thin muscles | | A medium build, moderately developed physique, good muscles | | Curvy, big boned, big build, or stocky, well-developed muscles | |
| **Weight** | Light and generally thin | | Moderate weight which remains more or less constant | | A tendency to gain weight | |
| **Hair** | Coarse, dry, and slightly wavy or frizzy hair | | Fine, soft hair or prematurely gray or bald | | Thick, oily, lustrous, or wavy hair | |
| **Head and face** | Small, thin, and long | | Moderate, ruddy, sharp contours | | Large, steady, round, pale, soft contours | |
| **Eyes** | Small, dry, and attractive | | Medium and penetrating | | Large and pleasant | |
| **Neck** | Thin, long | | Medium | | Large, thick | |
| **Skin** | Thin, dry, and cool; dull complexion | | Warm, moist, pink; prone to skin rashes | | Thick, smooth, moist, oily, soft | |
| **Mouth** | Gappy teeth, rough and cracked, receding gums, grind teeth | | Prone to bleeding gums, yellow teeth, can have bad breath | | Strong, round healthy teeth and gums | |
| **Features** | Small, thin, dry (e.g. lips) | | Medium | | Large, firm, soft | |
| **Hands and feet** (count separately) | Small, thin, dry, cold, and cracked, unsteady | | Medium, warm, healthy | | Large, thick, cool, firm | |
| **Legs and arms** (count separately) | Thin and small, overly long or short, prominent knees | | Medium | | Large, thick, well-developed arms, large or stocky legs | |
| **Nails** | Brittle, narrow | | Medium, soft | | Large, white, hard | |
| **Voice** | Low, weak, hoarse | | High pitched, moderate, sharp, good | | Pleasant, deep voice | |
| **Body strength** | Low, poor endurance | | Medium | | Strong with good stamina | |
| **Speech** | Erratic, enthusiastic, fast, and might miss out words | | Clear, sharp, and measured, logical | | Slow, resonant, clear, rhythmic | |

| | VATA ✔ | PITTA ✔ | KAPHA ✔ |
|---|---|---|---|
| **Personality** | Enthusiastic, lively, creative, and imaginative | Efficient and disciplined, analytical, driven, perfectionist, orderly | Loving, calm, patient, happy, supportive, home-loving |
| **Sociability** | Sometimes feels shy in social situations but can be very chatty | Outgoing and assertive | Sociable and make friends easily |
| **Character** | Likes to be active and busy | Organized and focused | Slow and methodical |
| **Ability to forgive** | Forgive and forget easily | Finds it hard to forgive | Forgives easily |
| **Activity** | Quick, unsteady, and distracted | Medium, motivated, competitive, focused | Slow, measured, deliberate, enjoys repetitive tasks |
| **Sexual nature and fertility** | Variable, low stamina, and low fertility | Moderate, passionate, domineering | Low but constant desire, good energy and fertility |
| **Immunity** | Variable, poor, and weak | Medium, prone to infection | Strong |
| **Disease tendency** | Nervous system, arthritis, severe stress, weakness, aches and pains | Skin rashes, inflammations, infections, fevers, acidity, heartburn | Bronchitis, asthma, allergies, congestion, obesity, high cholesterol |
| **Sweat** | Light and no smell | Profuse and strong smell | Moderate, cold, and mild smell |
| **Bowel movements** | Dry, tendency toward constipation and gas | Regular and loose, yellowish, tendency toward diarrhea | Regular, solid, and well formed |
| **Appetite** | Variable and erratic, sometimes large meals, moderate thirst | Strong and sharp, needs lots of food, rarely misses a meal, strong thirst | Constant, doesn't need much food but often craves it, not very thirsty |
| **Memory and learning** | Once focused, quick to grasp, good short-term memory but forgets quickly | Moderately quick to grasp, very good memory, rarely forgets | Takes time to grasp things but then never forgets |
| **Sleep** | Light, fitful sleep, wakes up early, lots of impressionable dreams | Moderate but good sleeper | Deep sleeper, finds it hard to get up in the morning |
| **Excitability** | Quick to rise but also fall | Quick to get excited but endures | Slow |
| **Emotions when stressed** | Tendency toward anxiety, worry, fear, nervousness | Tendency toward anger and irritation, jealousy | Tendency toward depression, and attachment, lack of motivation, self pity, greed |
| **Money** | Impulsive spender | Considered spender, enjoys luxuries and gourmet meals | Reluctant spender, likes to save but spends on food, entertainment, and property |
| **Walking** | Fast and erratic | Fast but steady | Slow and steady |
| **Professions** | Artists, philosophers, communicators, organizers, models, actors | Leaders, brokers, self-employed, analysis, politics, education | Nurturers, carers, nurses, cooks, self-employed business people |
| **Mental nature** | Quick, adaptable but indecisive | Intelligent, critical, decisive, loves logic and structure | Slow, steady, sensitive |
| **Religion** | Erratic, changeable | Focused, fanatic | Constant, loyal, conservative |
| **Recreation** | Likes speed, traveling, dancing, plays, parks, artistic endeavors | Likes competitive sports, politics, debates, research, hunting | Likes flowers, sailing, eating out or cooking, watching movies, reading |
| TOTAL | | | |

# Qualities of The Doshas

To manage health through the elements, we need to be able to identify them in everyday life. As we have seen, we identify them through their inherent qualities. In the body, they can be seen on a physical, mental, and emotional level.

## The Vata Dosha

The qualities of vata are those of air and ether—light, dry, rough, clear, active, and cold. If you are a natural vata, you will probably have similar qualities—a light build, little body fat, light sleep, dry, rough skin and hair, be very active, and see things quite clearly. These are very simple examples, but these qualities extend to all parts of our physiology and personality. In the body, vata governs all movement, including breathing, blinking, and circulation. In nature, anything with a predominance of one or more of these qualities will have a large amount of air and ether in them, e.g. the season of fall, cookie crackers, exercise.

## The Pitta Dosha

The qualities of pitta are those of fire with a little water—hot, slightly viscous, sharp, burning, penetrating, and acidic. Pitta is often compared to gasoline—it is liquid and flammable, but not the flame itself. A person who is a pitta body type will have a hot temperament, sharp and penetrating mind and speech, and a strong digestive system. In the body, pitta gives us our body temperature and our acids and enzymes, which help us digest both food and information. Anything with any of these qualities will have a predominance of fire or pitta, e.g. summer, chiles, vinegar.

## The Kapha Dosha

The qualities of the kapha dosha are those of earth and water—heavy, stable, cold, smooth, slow, soft, oily, and moist. Kapha, being earth and water, forms all the tissues and organs of the body, as well as all the moisture or water in and between the cells. People with a kapha body type are normally heavier in build, and are stable characters who dislike too much activity or change. They have smooth, soft, and oily skin and healthy, thick hair. Anything with these qualities will have a predominance of kapha, such as the season of winter, ice cream, even a sedentary job.

# Balance and Health

Dosha means "fault" and in a sense this is an apt translation, as our dosha indicates an excess of one or two of the elements in our body. If left unchecked, this element will be the first to increase to an imbalance, with a prolonged imbalance leading to illness. Health is, therefore, achieved by keeping our doshas balanced.

When our doshas are balanced, whether you are naturally pitta, kapha, or vata, we are the best version of ourselves. We will have our quirks and our issues but will be healthy and happy. When our dominant dosha increases, we become extreme versions of ourselves or imbalanced. For example, a vata person who is active can become restless, distracted, and overactive. A kapha person who is slow and measured might become lazy, inactive, or depressed. A pitta person who is critical and organized might become controlling and dominating.

If, on the other hand, we imbalance one of the other doshas (not our dominant one), this is called vikriti. This often happens following a deliberate change in your natural or normal lifestyle. For instance, a pitta or kapha person on a diet and exercise program to lose weight will be increasing the vata dosha in themselves (taking in the main qualities of vata—lightness of food and body, and being active). This increase could then lead to a vata imbalance and may result in different health issues. Regardless of your own dosha, any current imbalance needs to be addressed and corrected first.

A prolonged imbalance in our doshas will lead to illness so it is important to identify your own dosha(s). The dosha questionnaire (see pages 10–11) will help you recognize which dosha is the predominant one. I would advise you to complete the questionnaire twice, firstly with an eye to your natural constitution, who you are in your most natural state (I think back to childhood, which is untainted by outside conditioning), and secondly with an eye to how you are now in order to find your vikriti or current imbalance.

## "Natural forces within us are the true healers of disease." Hippocrates

# Ayurveda and the Body

Ayurveda sees our body as a composition of seven types of tissue—plasma, blood, muscle, fat, bone, marrow, and nerve, and reproductive tissues. These are served by a complex network of channels which carry nutrients to them. A subtle network of channels carries prana, "primal breath" or our life force, around the body. There are also seven energy centers, chakras, which start at the base of the spine and go up to the top of our head.

Along with this, our body has a digestive and metabolic system, agni. Food is our fuel and our agni breaks it down into its nutrient parts. These nutrients will then nourish the seven tissues one after the other, as if they are concentric circles with plasma as the first outer tissue, then nourishing the rest one after the other, ending with the reproductive tissues. As each tissue is nourished, the nutrients are refined and a by-product is produced, such as hair or nails. The nutrients are therefore refined seven times (with each tissue) and there are seven by-products. The substance you are finally left with is called ojas and is best described as the happy/bliss energy and is connected with good immunity.

## Agni—Our Digestive Fire

Agni loosely translates as "fire" and it encompasses both digestion and metabolism. Unfortunately, we rarely pay much attention to our digestive system anymore, taking it for granted and assuming it is healthy and working properly. When we get indigestion, gas, or acidity, we shrug and take a pill to alleviate the symptoms, never looking deeper. Ayurvedic doctors believe that the secret to good health lies in a healthy agni.

## An Unhealthy Agni

When your digestive system is healthy, you will have good digestion, circulation, and complexion and high levels of energy and immunity. A weak agni cannot properly digest the food you eat and some parts of your meal will remain undigested in the gut. As a result, you will not be absorbing all the nutrients from your food but, more importantly, as the undigested food sits in the gut, it will produce toxins, known as ama.

Ama is sticky by nature and will initially accumulate in the gut, but eventually it will overflow into the rest of the body. In doing so, it can clog channels such as the intestines, lymphatic system, respiratory tract, and arteries, and also the subtle channels which move energy around the body. This can cause a hormonal imbalance and weight gain and can often accumulate in an area of the body that is already weak, such as an organ or bones, resulting in serious illnesses.

Ama is considered the root of all illness and I cannot overstate how detrimental a toxic buildup can be. If you feel you have a toxic buildup, read the section on detox (see page 46).

Regardless of whether our agni is strong, erratic, or low, we need to make sure we take care of it so that it remains healthy.

Symptoms of an ama buildup include:

- A feeling of heaviness, lethargy, and dullness
- It will affect your mental clarity so you will feel unfocused or unclear
- Being bloated and windy
- Aches and stiffness in your hips and back
- Ama has a foul odor which comes out in breath, sweat, and bodily excretions
- A coated tongue in the morning and a sticky, sweet taste in the mouth
- The sense of having "lost your mojo"

## Agni and the Doshas

Not everyone's agni (even if healthy) is as efficient as the next; your dosha can affect your agni in the same way as the elements can affect a flame.

- The fire element in pitta adds intensity to agni's own heat so pitta body types naturally have strong digestions and metabolism. When pitta is balanced, they are strong, healthy, and rarely gain weight. An imbalanced pitta person will have a tendency toward suffering hyperacidity, gastritis, heartburn, and diarrhea.

- The affect of excess vata on the agni is almost like the effects of wind on fire—sometimes it is quiet and the flame burns well, but at other times it agitates the flame, making it flicker or burn off course. So vata body types are said to have erratic digestive systems and have to try to eat easy-to-digest foods and not overburden their system. An imbalanced vata person might have irregular appetites, indigestion, bloating, and wind.

- Earth and water act on agni as they would on an actual fire, they dampen it causing it to burn with a decreased intensity. This low agni is the main reason kapha people have a tendency toward weight gain; they have a slow metabolism. When a kapha person is imbalanced, they will have a tendency to feel sluggish and slow, heavy, and congested.

## Maintaining a Healthy Agni

Eating in a way which continually puts a strain on your digestive system will eventually weaken it. Overeating, hard-to-digest, or unnatural foods and erratic eating will all strain your digestion.

- Eat in a way which is good for your body type (see pages 26, 32, and 38 on balancing doshas).

- Eat only once you are sure you have digested your last meal. A primitive but effective way of being sure that your stomach is clear is to drink some hot water. When you belch (obviously in private!), if it smells of food, it is still in your stomach.

- Eat meals at regular times each day. If you are not hungry, delay a little but try to maintain a routine.

- Do not skip meals or undereat; erratic eating weakens agni (as shown by yo-yo dieting which lowers metabolism).

- Eat when calm and without too much distraction. Eating when stressed, depressed, upset, or just on-the-go will hamper or strain digestion. Ideally focus on what you are eating.

- Reduce the amount of overly spiced meals, heavy foods, dairy products, and alcohol as they all hamper proper digestion.

- Do not overeat (even healthy foods) as this will overload agni. Ideally, we should eat until we are only 50 percent full for proper digestion to take place.

- Copy the Chinese by only sipping hot herbal tea or water with your meals. Ideally, do not drink a full glass of water 30 minutes before your meal and for 1 hour afterward as water dilutes the acids in the stomach.

- Drink hot water or herbal or spice teas throughout the day as they strengthen agni.

- Raw food is harder to digest than cooked food, so make sure you mostly eat cooked meals (pitta can eat raw food as they have strong digestive systems).

- Pregnancy, menstruation, menopause, and medicine all affect agni, so be kind to your digestion at these times by eating light food.

- Exercising to a moderate intensity helps strengthen your digestive system.

## Food Combining

Ayurveda believes that different foods often require different digestive enzymes, meaning that certain foods do not combine well in the stomach. These combinations, called antagonistic foods, are best not eaten together. The main combinations to avoid are:

- Do not mix milk with sour ingredients such as tomatoes, yogurt, and acidic fruits (so no more strawberry milkshakes!).

- Fresh fruit should be eaten by itself, separate from meals (dried or cooked fruits are fine though), as it will not digest properly with other foods.

- Avoid mixing different types of proteins in one meal, such as fish and cheese or meat and beans, as these are hard to digest and two of them might overburden your agni.

- We digest tastes in an order: sweet, salty, sour, pungent, bitter, and astringent. If we eat all these tastes in one meal, our bodies will digest them in the right order and all will be fine. However, if you eat a meal and follow with dessert 15 minutes later, your digestive system has to start at the beginning again and this can overwork agni. A small amount of dessert is fine occasionally, but perhaps try eating a small lunch and if you get hungry midafternoon, have a small sweet snack then.

I know this might be a lot to take in but the more you do, the better you feel and you will find feeling good is addictive. Get in touch (and stay in touch) with your digestion. Be aware of your hunger levels, as you are the only one who will know how much and when to eat.

# The Doshas: In and Out of Balance

| | Vata  | Pitta  | Kapha  |
|---|---|---|---|
| Qualities | Light, dry, rough, clear, active, cold | Hot, slightly viscous, sharp, burning, penetrating, acidic | Heavy, stable, cold, smooth, slow, soft, oily, sticky, moist |
| When balanced | Happy, energetic, vibrant, enthusiastic, clear and active mind, creative, adaptive, imaginative, innovative, sensitive, talkative | Content, happy, enjoys challenges and debates, sharp mind and able to focus easily, good orator, bold, witty, intellectual, strong digestion, glowing complexion | Family orientated, affectionate, loving, loyal, compassionate, forgiving, stable, relaxed, slow and methodical, good memory, good stamina |
| Imbalanced | Weight loss, overactive and restless, disturbed sleep, physically tired and weak, anxious, lots of nervous energy, bad memory | Aggressive, competitive, critical, demanding, perfectionist, angry, irritable and impatient, prematurely graying hair or hair loss | Lazy and inactive, dull, oily skin, slow digestion, lethargic, possessive, overattached, tendency to oversleep, overweight |
| Aggravating factors | Being overactive, not sleeping enough, stress, too many bitter, astringent, and pungent foods, undereating or irregular meals, irregular routine, too much exercise, traveling or stimulation; fall weather can also cause a minor vata imbalance | Stress, being in the heat for too long, drinking too much, smoking, missing meals, eating too much spicy, sour, or salty food, hot and summery weather or being in a hot environment can cause a minor pitta imbalance | Oversleeping and being really inactive, overeating, emotional eating, being stuck in a rut with few new experiences, eating too many sweet, sour, or salty foods, or cold, wet wintry weather can cause a minor kapha imbalance |

Sweet

Salty

Sour

Bitter

Astringent

Pungent

# Eating the Ayurvedic Way

Ayurveda sees food as nourishing, balancing, and healing. Food is one of the few aspects of our health that we have almost total control over so it is vital to have a better understanding of what we eat. Food comprises the same five elements as our bodies: water, earth, air, ether, and fire. Knowing the element(s) in foods means we can choose ingredients to help balance our own doshas or reduce intake of those which will lead to an imbalance. In the body, the elements become doshas; in food they are defined as tastes. There are six tastes and, as with the doshas, they all have separate functions in the body.

## Sweet

Earth and water are the predominant elements of this taste and its qualities are heavy, moist, and oily. Sweet refers to the inherent sweetness in fats, meat, grains, starchy veg, fruit, milk, beans, and nuts. This taste should form the bulk of our diet as it nourishes the body's tissues and, in moderation, increases strength and immunity, is grounding, and promotes happiness and peace. It's a great taste for vata and is also good for pitta. Kapha need to be more careful as they share the same elements and, in excess, this can lead to heaviness, bulk, congestion, and mucus.

## Sour

Fire is the predominant element, but there is a little earth and water. It is heating and somewhat heavy and moistening. In moderation, it nourishes all but the reproductive tissues (with the exception of yogurt which does), stimulates digestion, strengthens the heart, and sharpens the senses. Sour foods include vinegars, tamarind, tomatoes, yogurt, yellow cheeses, alcohol, pickles, and sour fruits. Sour foods easily imbalance pitta so should largely be avoided, and in excess they will aggravate kapha as it is heavy and moistening. It is a good taste for balancing vata.

## Bitter

This taste is made of the air and ether elements and its qualities are cold, light, and dry. It is cleansing and detoxifying, improves appetite and digestion, is good for weight loss, and keeps the skin firm. This flavor is found in many herbs, green vegetables like kale or endive, fruits such as grapefruit, caffeine, and certain spices such as fenugreek and turmeric. Bitter foods should be eaten only in small quantities as their properties are strong. This taste is great for balancing kapha and pitta types, but should be eaten sparingly by vata.

## Salty

This taste is made up of water and fire and is heavy, hot, moist, and pungent. In moderation, it improves digestion, lubricates tissues, and calms the nerves. An excess of salt in our diet may cause hyperacidity and dryness in skin and hair (leading to wrinkles, hair loss, and high blood pressure). This taste is good for vata, but will increase both pitta as it is heating and kapha because it is heavy and moist. Salt comes in the form of sea and rock salt, seaweed and soy sauce. Ayurveda's salt of choice is rock salt.

## Astringent

This taste is made up of earth and air and is dry, cooling, and slightly heavy. It is less of a taste and more of an effect; it makes the mouth pucker and feel dry. Tannins (tea, red wine) are obviously astringent, but so too are many green vegetables such as broccoli, cauliflower, artichoke, and asparagus. Cranberries, pomegranates, pears, and apples all have a degree of astringency, as do beans and lentils. Old honey (over six months old) is also astringent. Too many astringent foods can cause a vata imbalance but are very good for kapha and pitta.

## Pungent

The elements here are fire and air, and it is light, heating, and drying. It is stimulating, reduces gas and inflammation, strengthens agni, helps burn ama, clears sinuses, and helps with obesity, diabetes, high cholesterol, and circulation. Raw onions and garlic, chiles, ginger, radishes, arugula, and strong spices have a pungent taste, but should be eaten in small quantities as they are powerful. It is a great taste for kapha who should try to incorporate pungency into their meals every day. Apart from the spices, it is not great for vata. Pitta should eat only a little of the mildest of spices.

| Taste | Elements | Qualities | Vata | Pitta | Kapha |
|---|---|---|---|---|---|
| Sweet | Earth and Water | Cool, moistening, heavy | Reduces | Reduces | Really increases |
| Sour | Fire and Earth | Hot, slightly, heavy, and slightly moist | Reduces | Really increases | Increases |
| Salty | Water and Fire | Quite hot, heavy, moistening | Reduces | Increases | Increases |
| Bitter | Air and Ether | Cool, light, drying | Increases | Reduces | Really reduces |
| Pungent | Fire and Air | Very hot, light, very drying | Increases a little | Really increases | Really reduces |
| Astringent | Earth and Air | Cool, a little heavy, and slightly drying | Increases | Reduces | Reduces |

Hunger tells us that our body needs nutrients but we do not know which ones. Including all six tastes in our daily diet and eating a variety of foods will ensure that we meet all our body's needs for strength and proper functioning. But we do need to be careful of those tastes which share the same dominant elements as ourselves or our current imbalance. Serious illnesses do not develop overnight, they come about by eating the wrong food for your body day after day, for years. As most of us get stuck in food ruts and repeat the same meals, we are all in danger of an imbalance.

# Food and the Spirit

Ayurveda believes that the food we eat breaks down to three parts in the body; the gross part is waste to be eliminated, the middle part contains the nutrients, and the last part consists of subtle energies which affect who we are. These are sometimes known as doshas of the mind, but are really more about our spirit. There are three of these vibrations, or gunas.

### Rajasic—*stimulation, activity, passion, creativity*

Pungent, sour, and salty flavors are rajasic. Rajasic food is stimulating, it gives energy but in excess causes aggression and competitiveness. Unfortunately, the tastiest food is rajasic. Heavy, salty breads, caffeinated drinks, roasted nuts, deep-fried foods, and tangy vegetables are all rajasic. All meat and alcohol, in small amounts, are rajasic but in excess they are tamasic (see right). This makes sense as a little alcohol makes us animated but too much leads to depression and inertia. Eat rajasic foods in moderation.

### Tamasic— *dullness, inertia, heaviness, darkness, and attachment*

Eating tamasic food can lead to confusion, pessimism, greed, dullness, and lethargy. Foods in this category have little vitality, for example canned and frozen foods, dried milk powder, leftovers, and processed foods. Food cooked in the microwave, past its expiration date, pan-fried foods, mushrooms, lots of alcohol or meat, and drugs are all tamasic. These foods should be avoided as much as possible.

### Sattvic—*clarity, peace, and happiness*

Eating a sattvic diet keeps our minds pure and clear and gives us health, peace, and contentment. These foods are wholesome and easy to digest. Meals are cooked and eaten in small portions and the diet would consist of whole grains, small lentils, milk, ghee, most vegetables, fruits, and raw nuts.

# How We Eat in the West

We are always striving to eat better food and make healthier choices, but I doubt many of us realize exactly how harmful it can be to consistently eat the wrong foods. In the West, our diet is often replete with processed, refined convenience and fast foods which are mainly sweet, salty, and sour in taste. Even homemade meals, by and large, shun pungent, bitter, and astringent tastes for more palatable ones. When we are stressed, we instinctively graze on refined sugary snacks to calm our nerves or have an evening drink (cocktails may taste sweet, but all alcohol is sour).

This imbalance of tastes, coupled with our sedentary lifestyle, often leads to a kapha imbalance which can be seen in the increasing levels of obesity, diabetes, asthma, and heart conditions. We also consume a lot of rajasic and tamasic foods/drinks and the effects of this are reflected in the high levels of aggression, competitiveness, dissatisfaction, and depression around us.

## Buddha says "Every human being is the author of his own health or disease."

Fresh, wholesome meals which include pungent, bitter, and astringent tastes, like a simple meal of rice, spiced beans, and greens, will quickly reinstate balance. They are also cleansing and detoxifying. We see what happens to children when they are switched from a bad diet to one of freshly cooked meals—their concentration, clarity, and temperament all improve. It isn't rocket science; our body gets everything it needs from the nutrients we eat, so an intake of too few nutrients means something will suffer.

# Embracing the Ayurvedic Food Journey

It is important to remember that what you eat is as important as being able to digest and absorb the nutrients in it. Ayurveda is very particular about both food and proper digestion. Here are a few simple and logical guidelines that serve as a gentle reminder as to how we should be eating for maximum nutrition and health.

• Your body is your temple. Try to opt for food that is 100 percent natural, organic, preservative-free, and chemical-free, with no artificial additives or sweeteners. Limit your intake of processed, canned, and frozen foods. Try to eat seasonally, with warming food in the winter and cooling meals in the summer.

• Eat at regular times every day, as erratic eating patterns and skipping meals weaken your digestion and metabolism. The digestive system is strongest at lunchtime, so make this your biggest meal.

• Try to eat simply with few ingredients on your plate. The more complex your meal, the harder it is for your system to process.

• Do not eat anything until you have digested your last meal (see page 15).

• Do not overeat, this overburdens your digestive system and will lead to some indigestion and create ama. We should eat until we are 50 percent full for the most efficient digestion.

• Eating when stressed, on the go, or when overly stimulated will hamper digestion. Eat when calm and seated, without distraction, stress, or anxiety.

• Ideally, sip hot water with your meals, as it is great for digestion. Drinking too much or drinking cold drinks will hamper digestion.

• Fresh fruit should be eaten alone, away from other food. Small amounts of soaked dried fruits and cooked fruits can be taken with other foods.

• Milk should ideally be drunk on its own and preferably warm and lightly spiced, but it also goes well with grains, as in an oatmeal or rice dessert. If you take it with a meal, such as breakfast, do not partner it with sour foods.

• Avoid eating sour foods such as yogurt, cheese, and sour fruits after 5pm.

• Make sure you eat food which is good for your body and include, but monitor, all six tastes (see pages 19–20).

# The Vata Dosha

Being born with a **vata** constitution means you are blessed with the all-elusive slender figure—you are the natural supermodel! You have an endearing quality and are creative, sensitive, and friendly. You like to sing, dance, are artistic, and life is always busy and full. Typical characteristics of a healthy vata body type are:

- You are naturally slim, often with a small frame with a prominent collarbone, delicate arms, and slightly jutting bones.

- You are enthusiastic about life, lively, and talk animatedly.

- You are always on the go and even walk fast, though often erratically.

- Like the wind, you are adaptable and flexible, but can be a little indecisive too.

- You are cheerful, but sometimes a little shy in new situations.

- Physically, you have a tendency toward dryness and often have dry but full or coarse hair.

- You are a quick thinker, learn quickly but also have a tendency to forget easily.

- You are often intuitive.

- You have a great work ethic and make a fantastic employee as you work hard and get the job done on time, as long as you don't get distracted first. You are determined and trustworthy.

- You are creative, sensitive, and imaginative.

- You spend money freely on having a good time and whatever else you fancy, but you do get nervous about your money running out before the next paycheck.

- Like a new mom, you sleep lightly and often have impressionable dreams (often of flying).

- You love the warmth as you feel the cold quickly and often have cold hands and feet.

- In the event that you do put on weight, it normally settles around your waist.

When you are balanced, you are enthusiastic about life and love traveling, speed, and stimulating pursuits, as well as artistic activities and creative outlets like plays and novels.

# A Vata Imbalance

In Ayurveda, like increases like, so if you live a life and eat a diet which increases the cold, light, dry, rough, and active qualities of vata, you will increase this element in your body. Being born with a vata constitution does not mean you have a vata imbalance, only that you are more susceptible to one—anyone can develop a vata imbalance when their diet and lifestyle increase these qualities.

An imbalance can come about from one or a combination of:

- Undereating or eating erratically will increase vata.

- Being continually stressed, anxious, or overstimulated.

- Being overactive, over-exercising, not sleeping enough, or traveling excessively.

- Constantly eating food with dry, rough, light, cold properties such as salads, raw vegetables, crackers, or eating "windy" foods like beans.

- Vata increases over 60, so we see an increase in osteoporosis (air in the bones) and wrinkling (drying) skin and brittle hair.

- Dry, cold, and windy weather can exasperate a vata imbalance (dress appropriately).

- After a woman gives birth, her vata is imbalanced and her tissues depleted so in India a new mother is fed nourishing foods to bring vata down and replenish tissues.

Living in the twenty-first century can easily imbalance vata, as we are forever overcommitting and over-extending ourselves. We accept the levels of stress that come with modern life but don't always manage this stress well. We strive for thinness by living on salads and vegetables and doing lots of exercise, all of which increase vata. We travel a lot and generally live life going from one stimulating environment to another.

Signs of a vata imbalance are:

- Your skin, lips, and eyes become dry and your hair and nails become brittle.

- You feel more nervous, fearful, stressed, depressed, anxious, and have tension headaches.

- You become increasingly shy, self-defeating, and insecure.

- You may suffer from insomnia and light, fitful sleep.

- You have poor circulation, cold hands and feet.

- Joint pains, lower back pain, and bone problems, such as arthritis or osteoporosis, may occur.

- You feel restless and impatient. You find it hard to focus and make decisions, and you feel spaced out or ungrounded.

- You often feel bloated and suffer excessive wind.

- You become more constipated than is normal for your body.

- You have a low and irregular appetite and lose weight.

- You are easily fatigued but still feel the need to be active.

- Women may have light or irregular periods or amenorrhea.

If you have a vata imbalance, identify the reasons for it, and really focus on changing or resolving them while you follow the vata-balancing diet and lifestyle (see pages 26–28) until you feel more balanced.

# The Vata-Balancing Diet

To balance vata, eat a nourishing, warming, and comforting diet. Eating the right ingredients is as important as how you cook them, how much you eat, and how well you digest them. Vata body types sometimes find it hard to digest a large, heavy meal (which is what they need), so eating small portions of nutrient-dense foods is recommended. Follow these guidelines and use the food charts on pages 153–158 to see which ingredients are best and vary the ingredients for maximum nutrition.

• Vata have an erratic digestive fire (as if the excess air in your body agitates the fire, making it flicker). To avoid indigestion and ama, eat small portions of simple food (the more ingredients on your plate, the harder they will be to digest). Your meals should be cooked and ideally served warm, including your breakfast.

• Be careful not to overeat at any meal, eat only when you feel hungry and the last meal has been digested (see page 15).

• Eat at regular times everyday. Your digestive fire is strongest at 1pm so lunch like a king or queen. Erratic eating like skipping meals will aggravate vata and then when you do eat, you often over-eat which will overload your agni.

• Eat when you are calm. For efficient digestion, avoid eating when stressed, anxious, over-stimulated, or distracted.

• Your meals should be creamy, unctuous, moist, and smooth, and cooked with ghee, oil, or cream. Comfort food is good for vata physically and emotionally, so include soup, stews, rice desserts, risottos, lentils, rice, pasta, or curry.

• Eat natural foods and avoid all processed or fried foods, "windy" beans and vegetables, cold, raw food, or dry food, such as crackers or cereal. If you love salads, eat them mainly in the summer and well dressed with oil.

• Focus on foods which are sweet, sour, and salty and reduce your consumption of bitter, astringent, and pungent tastes (with the exception of spices which in moderation will help strengthen the digestive system).

• Rice and wheat are the best grains for you, followed by oats. Mung and red lentils are good, as is tofu (if you can digest it).

• Sweet fruits are good, but dried fruits can cause gas, so avoid unless well soaked.

• Avoid too many nuts as they can be hard to digest. Soak them to soften or grind and add to your food.

• Avoid caffeine as it is stimulating, and also cold and carbonated drinks. Opt instead for herbal teas, hot water, or warm milk. Masala tea is okay as it is warming and milky. The occasional alcoholic drink to help you unwind is fine. Warm milk spiced with cardamom, cinnamon, and nutmeg before bedtime is calming and will help with sleep.

• Vata can snack if hungry between meals, but be careful as many convenient snacks tend to be drying, such as crackers, potato chips, and cereal bars. Try fruits, lassi (see page 152), or a small handful of soaked or well-chewed nuts.

Enjoy your food. It gives you nourishment and good health, and keeps you balanced. It is one of life's pleasures.

# A Vata-Balancing Lifestyle

The way to balance vata seems, to me, the nicest way of living. Unfortunately, for most vata body types it is something they already know but cannot help themselves. Key actions for you are to slow down, relax, nourish, and ground yourself. Follow these guidelines for balancing vata.

• Establish a daily routine, waking, eating, and sleeping at roughly the same time each day.

• Be aware of not overexerting yourself through your activities. Strenuous exercise, competitive or speed sports, and aerobics will increase the air element in the body. Practice yoga, go for a walk (ideally in natural surroundings), dance, or swim.

• Try out some new creative hobbies, such as writing or painting, and don't spend all your free time sitting in front of the computer or TV.

• Learn how to manage your tendencies toward stress, anxiety, and restlessness. Meditation (even just 5 to 10 minutes each day), yoga, tai chi, a walk in the park, a drink and chat with a friend, listening to music, a swim, or even just sitting still in nature will all help calm you. Breathing exercises (pranayama) are particularly good as they are very relaxing and also help to control the breath (air) in the body.

• Daily massages with light massage oils are a great way to counter dry skin.

• Sleep is really important for all doshas but particularly for vata as you often have interrupted sleep. Try to get to bed early and drink a cup of lightly spiced (nutmeg, cinnamon, cardamom) warm milk.

• Cut back on excessive travel, overworking, overstimulation, and even overthinking (creates more stress and anxiety). Find ways of slowing down, calming down, and grounding yourself.

• Wrap up warm in cold weather and avoid being in air conditioning for too long.

I know that it is really hard to see how you can slow down when your life is always running at full tilt, but I have found that it is amazing how, if you take on a little less every day and make a little "you" time, things still get done, life does not collapse around us and everyone we love gets used to the new routine very soon.

# Menu Plan for Vata

### Monday
Vitality oatmeal, page **63**
Mom's chicken stew with a hunk
of buttered bread, page **71**
Zucchini, basil, and goat cheese
carbonara, page **134**

### Tuesday
Cardamom-laced semolina, page **59**
South Indian haddock and corn
chowder, page **75**
Cooling coconut and lemon cupcake
with a cup of tea, page **143**
Risotto with pumpkin seed, mint, and
fava bean pesto, page **125**

### Wednesday
Spiced fruit compote, page **67**
Chicken, fennel, and fava bean salad,
page **93**
Greek-style chicken with lemon,
potatoes, and garlic, page **114**

### Thursday
Lemon and blueberry cornmeal
pancakes, with a little butter and
drizzled with maple syrup, page **60**
Hearty lentil and herb soup, page **72**
Provençal trout with lemon salsa
verde and some seasonal vegetables,
page **103**

### Friday
Quinoa and sweet spice oatmeal,
page **63**
Warm sweet potato, arugula, and
goat cheese salad, page **84**
Almond, orange, and fennel seed
biscotti, page **147**, with a cup of
masala chai or tea, page **152**
Chicken, broccoli, and pea curry with
rice, page **107**

### Saturday
Asparagus and goat cheese frittata,
page **67**
Broiled sardines with "sauce vierge"
on toast and seasonal vegetables on
the side, page **103**
Chicken laksa with rice noodles,
page **117**
Slightly sticky date cake with jaggery
walnut toffee sauce, page **150**

### Sunday
Spicy scrambled tofu with toast,
page **64**
Ayurvedic lentil curry, page **128**, with
southern-style sautéed sweet
potatoes, page **133**, and rice
Moroccan-braised chicken with flat
bread, page **108**

Here is a general menu to give
you an idea of a week's worth of
meals. This is just a guide—you
can vary it as much as you like,
there are more recipes in this
book to choose from and there
are food charts on pages
153–158 to help you create your
own dishes. If you have an easy
working arrangement, definitely
make your lunch your main meal
but eat small portions of
nourishing food at all meals.

## Vata's pantry basics
Ghee, yellow mung lentils, red
lentils, green mung beans,
coconut milk, brown or white
long-grained rice, spelt flour,
quinoa, jaggery, spices, oats,
nuts, bulgur wheat, sesame
seeds/tahini.

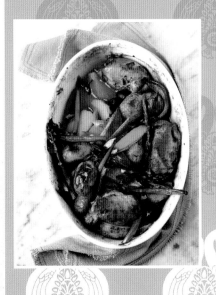

# The Pitta Dosha

Being born with a pitta constitution means you are blessed with a fantastic metabolism, a good physique, lots of energy, and are focused and organized. You are a natural leader and motivator, but also a sportsman and soldier.

Typical characteristics of a healthy pitta constitution are:

- You have a medium build with good muscle tone and a good complexion.

- You have a hearty appetite, are often quite thirsty, and enjoy cold foods.

- You enjoy good, sound sleep but not more than 8 hours (unless you are very hot).

- You are a good, strong orator, motivator, and leader.

- Although emotional, you are not necessarily sentimental.

- You are strong-willed, passionate, and goal orientated.

- You are entrepreneurial, inventive, and ambitious, determined and decisive.

- You are adventurous and brave and do what you set out to do.

- You are a clear thinker and have a sharp memory.

- You are intelligent and perceptive, but are also prone to being critical.

- Good with money, you don't spend on a whim.

- You are kind to friends but make a bad enemy.

- You have a tendency toward stress, irritation, and impatience, and anger.

- Your hair is prematurely graying or you suffer hair loss.

- When you become ill, you will have a tendency to suffer from inflammation, fever, skin and blood problems.

When you are balanced, you go through life focused and forge your own path. You are courageous, a thinker, and can be inventive.

# A Pitta Imbalance

In Ayurveda, like increases like so if you live a life and eat a diet which increases the hot, sharp, liquid, oily, and heavy qualities of pitta, you will increase this element in your body, which will lead to an imbalance. If you are a pitta body type, you are more susceptible to pitta imbalance, but anyone can develop one.

An imbalance can come about from being continually exposed to heat, whether it is the sun or working in a hot professional kitchen. Constantly eating food which is too sour, oily, sharp, and heating, such as tomatoes and vinegar, deep-fried foods, and very spicy food, will all unbalance pitta. Skipping meals will also aggravate your pitta.

The work environment is both competitive and stressful, which increases pitta. Even when we go out to unwind and shrug off the stresses of the day, we often do so with a drink, but alcohol is very sharp, penetrating, and sour and will compound the problem (if you look at alcoholics, many of their symptoms will be of those of an imbalanced pitta). Suppressing your emotions, especially those like anger and irritation, over a period of time will also increase pitta.

Signs of an imbalance are:

• You are constantly critical and judgmental of yourself and others.

• You feel the heat more than you usually do and sweat more than normal.

• You feel angry, irritated, or impatient, or controlling regularly.

• You feel you have lost clarity of thought as your passion and emotions cloud your judgment.

• You are becoming a workaholic and have lost the work–life balance.

• You are being quarrelsome, domineering, controlling, and even violent.

• You start to have disrupted, fitful sleep and disturbing dreams.

• You start feeling burned out.

• You have a lot of indigestion, heartburn, and acidity which can lead to stomach ulcers. You find you are experiencing diarrhea.

• You are getting skin rashes and inflammations. You have blood shot eyes, bad breath, and a sour body odor.

• You start to develop blood disorders and liver problems.

We are all predisposed to a mild pitta imbalance as we become adults and enter the workplace, so we need to remember to balance work life with play, family, and fun. If you have an imbalance, follow the balancing diet and lifestyle (see pages 32–34) until the problems clear up, then continue to follow loosely if you have a pitta constitution.

# The Pitta-Balancing Diet

You normally get away with eating whatever you want, but when pitta is out of balance it is a good idea to stick to the guidelines below. Meals need to be cooling and calming both in terms of ingredients and atmosphere. Use the food charts on pages 153–158 to select your best ingredients and eat a varied diet for maximum nutrition.

• Start cooking some of your meals with a little ghee (clarified butter) as it is a cooling fat while most oils are heating in nature (coconut oil is an exception as it is cooling).

• Sit down for a meal (but not at your desk); you need to eat in a calm environment.

• Focus on eating sweet, bitter, and astringent foods such as mung beans, coconut, cilantro, asparagus, sweet fruits, and salads.

• Salt, sourness, spices, and oil will all imbalance pitta, so your meals should be quite simple in taste. Avoid tomatoes, yogurt, vinegar, pickles, chiles, and yellow cheese.

• Foods should be cooling in nature, so opt for complex carbohydrates, fruits and fruit juices, milk, coconut, and root vegetables and salads.

• Meat, alcohol, and tobacco are heating. You should try to get most of your proteins from vegetable sources, such as mung beans and tofu. When you do eat meat, opt for lighter, white meats and avoid shellfish and egg yolks (whites are neutral).

• Don't skip a meal or go hungry. Snack between meals if necessary. Opt for crackers and oat cakes with some fresh soft white cheese or hummus. Organic cereal bars, crudités, fresh fruits, or milkshakes (vanilla ideally, as fruit and milk do not mix well). Dried fruit is good for you, especially dates as they cleanse the blood (imbalanced pitta can lead to blood disorders).

• Raw vegetables and salads suit you so include plenty of them in your diet, particularly in the summer, but stick to lemon-based dressings as this souring agent is more neutral than the rest.

• Avoid caffeine, black tea, and hot drinks in the summer. Drink water, warm herbal teas, sweet lassis, milk, and fruit juices instead. Pomegranate juice (see page 152) is fantastic for you.

# A Pitta-Balancing Lifestyle

I think our lifestyle habits are really hard to change but these changes are all so positive and fun. An imbalanced pitta will have a tendency toward irritation, impatience, anger, and competitiveness. The saying "getting hot under the collar" is exactly what happens to a person with too much heat in their tissues. The passionate pitta needs to stay cool, both physically and mentally.

• Don't sit in the sun for too long, especially if you have just eaten spicy food or have an empty stomach. And when you do sit in the sun, wear a hat.

• Do not overexercise (your body will overheat) and allow your body to cool down before going for a warm shower. Outdoor and water-based activities are great for you, but avoid sports which are overly competitive.

• Avoid saunas and steams as they will overheat the body.

• There are many techniques that can calm and cool the mind. Try meditation, yoga (with the exception of ashtanga and bikram yoga as both will add heat), tai chi, and cooling breathing exercises in the form of pranayama (yogic breathing exercises).

• Listen to calming music, take a walk in the park, by the sea or, even better, under the moonlight.

• Avoid angry and stressed people, cultivate peaceful emotions, and spend time with those you love and have fun with. Learning to rebalance your work life with family and friends, adding a little leisure and pleasure in your week is what you need. Avoid conflicts; be honest, modest, kind, and generous. Take time out to take a walk in a cool breeze, look around you at the best bits of nature, laugh a little, and understand how small things are often not worth getting ill over. Remember to take intelligent action in your life.

# Menu Plan for Pitta

## Monday
Quinoa and sweet spice oatmeal
page **63**
Southern Indian haddock and corn
chowder, page **75**, with a bread roll
Creamy salmon, potato, and bean
packages, page **96**

## Tuesday
White French toast with jaggery
walnuts, page **69**
Broiled endive, goat cheese, and beet
salad, page **89**, and some oat cakes
Fragrant coconut fish curry, page **99**,
with a simple rice pilaf, page **138**

## Wednesday
Cereal with milk
Warm eggplant, quinoa, and tofu
salad with ginger dressing, page **83**
Cooling coconut and lemon cupcake,
page **143**, with a cup of tea
Risotto with pumpkin seed, mint, and
fava bean pesto, page **125**

## Thursday
Vitality oatmeal, page **63**
Chicken, fennel, and fava bean salad,
page **93**
Winter squash, tofu, and tamari rice,
page **126**

## Friday
Spiced fruit compote, page **67**,
followed by toast
Warm cranberry bean, mozzarella,
and herb salad, page **88**
Almond, orange, and fennel seed
biscotti, page **147**, midafternoon
Persian chicken with saffron rice pilaf,
page **111**

## Saturday
Vitality oatmeal, page **63**
Fish and saffron stew with parsley
mayonnaise, page **95**, and some
bread
Moroccan braised chicken with dates
and vegetables, page **108**, and rice or
broiled spelt bread
Slightly sticky date cake with jaggery
walnut toffee sauce, page **150**

## Sunday
Lemon and blueberry cornmeal
pancakes, with a little butter and
maple syrup, page **60**
Middle Eastern meze plate, page **87**
Lentil and rice oatmeal (khicheri),
page **52** (to give your system
a break)

This is a generic menu to get you
started, but don't feel you have
to use it—eat as you please, as
long as you follow the guidelines.
Use the food charts on pages
153–158 to make up seasonal
meals that appeal to you. If you
have a hearty appetite, make
larger portions or start with
a simple soup or salad.

### Pitta's pantry basics
Rice, oats, quinoa, lentils, beans,
pearl barley, spelt flour, coconut
milk or dry unsweetened
coconut, granola or muesli,
pumpkin seeds, dried fruit, oat
cakes, ghee, unrefined sugar, pearl
barley, firm tofu, fruit juices like
pomegranate juice.

# The Kapha Dosha

Being born with a kapha constitution means you are blessed with a happy nature, are strong, healthy, and have good longevity. The qualities of kapha are heavy, stable, smooth, soft, oily, and moist. Kapha people are stable and give emotional support and love to people without judgment. The extra earth and water elements in your body make you that little bit more "earthy," but also act as a dampener on your agni so you have a slow metabolism.

Typical characteristics of a healthy kapha constitution are:

• Curvy with heavier frames, bigger bones, strong muscles, and a little extra body fat.

• You have good stamina, strength, and stability. You have moderate amounts of energy and act slowly and steadily.

• You are generous, warm, maternal, and patient by nature. You form good friendships and are a loyal and patient friend.

• Kapha people often stay close to their family, culture, and religion. You are calm, content, affectionate, sentimental, and romantic.

• You have good skin and nails and healthy, thick hair.

• You have a harmonious voice and speak slowly and steadily.

• You sleep well and have difficulty waking up in the morning.

• You make great employers, have empathy for people, and are good at making and saving money.

• You are very fertile; this is why women with "child-bearing hips" were prized.

• You are intelligent and although you might take some time to grasp a concept, you never forget it.

• You are prone to mucus, sinus problems, respiratory disorders, and weight gain.

• You have a tendency toward attachment to people, habits, or things.

• You love beautiful objects, flowers, cosmetics, and cooking.

# A Kapha Imbalance

Being kapha does not mean you have a kapha imbalance, only that you are more susceptible to one. A kapha imbalance can develop by living a life and eating a diet which has heavy, cold, dense, moist, stable, and slow qualities, and being inactive. A mild imbalance can happen during the winter, but we naturally counter it by eating warm foods and keeping warm. A real imbalance comes mainly from diet and lifestyle. Consistently eating foods which are heavy, oily, cold, and damp or sweet, sour, and salty will increase kapha.

Symptoms of a kapha imbalance are:

- Gaining weight, even though you are not eating more.

- Having frequent congestion, sinus problems, asthma, or colds.

- You feel tired and lazy, even though you are not being overactive. You are feeling a little depressed or melancholic.

- Poor digestion leading to a feeling of heaviness and lethargy after eating.

- You have painful or swollen joints, and your hair and skin feels oilier than usual.

- You feel like sleeping a lot and have difficulty waking up. You feel unmotivated and have a lack of desire and passion.

- You've become possessive, greedy, and attached to people and things and will hoard possessions.

- Polycystic ovary syndrome, hypothyroidism, and diabetes are often signs of an imbalanced kapha.

Those with a kapha imbalance should follow the kapha-balancing diet and lifestyle guidelines. Those born with a kapha constitution should keep an eye on their diet to ensure they are not eating too many kapha-imbalancing foods.

Anyone can develop a kapha imbalance by living a life and eating a diet which has heavy, cold, dense, moist, stable, and slow qualities.

# The Kapha-Balancing Diet

You should eat a light diet of freshly cooked, warm meals and small portion sizes. Follow the guidelines and use the food charts on pages 153–158 to discover which ingredients are best for you. Eat a varied diet for maximum nutrition.

- Kapha people do not need animal protein as they do not require the extra nourishment and it is both heavy and hard to digest. But of all the meats, chicken and turkey and some white-fleshed fish are the lightest and can be eaten in moderation. Choose vegetarian proteins such as beans, lentils, and tofu.

- Up your intake of bitter foods (salad greens, endives), astringent foods (apples and beans), and pungent foods (spices), and reduce the amount of sweet, sour, and salty foods in your diet.

- Eat freshly cooked, warm, and light meals that are a little dry in quality and cooked with little fat.

- Raw salads are hard to digest, so they should be eaten only in the summer and at lunchtime.

- Avoid all refined sugar products, yeasted breads, alcohol, and deep-fried foods. Be wary of low-fat products as they can be high in sugar.

- Dairy products are heavy and cold so are not a good for kapha. Stick to rice, soy, or even goat's milk, which is lighter. Cottage cheese and goat cheese are fine occasionally, but monitor how you feel after eating them (do they make your sinuses flair up?).

- Eat small portions, don't eat between meals, and don't eat your next meal until the last one has been digested (see page 15). Make lunch your biggest meal.

- Avoid cold and sodas. Drink spiced teas and, in the summer, spiced lassis (see page 152) to cleanse tissues and improve digestion.

- Avoid whole nuts as much as possible; grind them or opt for pumpkin and sunflower seeds.

- Find a way to stop yourself turning to food when stressed.

# A Kapha-Balancing Lifestyle

Those with a kapha imbalance often need something dramatic to happen to push themselves out of their comfort zone and make changes in their lifestyle. I know how difficult it is to adopt a new routine but you will definitely feel so much better for it. Even small changes will mount up and the effects should spur you on to make bigger ones. Try to embrace as many of these lifestyle changes as you can.

• Up your activity levels—you have the strength and stamina to do lots of cardiovascular exercise. It will help you maintain your weight and strengthen your agni. Light jogging (joints permitting), aerobics, or sports are ideal, but even a brisk walk will help. At work, avoid sitting too long, take the stairs, and walk wherever you can. Ashtanga, an active form of yoga, is very good for kapha.

• The sun is great for kapha body-types, as are steams and saunas. Spend time outdoors and don't sit in the air conditioning for too long. Take a hot bath or do a quick steam at home to alleviate blocked sinuses (place a towel over your head, bent over a pan of steaming water—it's cheap and effective).

• Those with a kapha imbalance may find they have a tendency to form attachments to people, objects, or habits. You can become dependent on them and sometimes find yourself stuck in an unhappy situation. This can prevent you moving on from bad jobs or relationships. Regular meditation will help shift this stagnant energy, as will pranayama breathing (see right). Declutter your house and take up some new hobbies.

• Sleep increases kapha so avoid napping in the day, wake up early, and throw yourself into a fun and busy day.

• Doing a liquid fast, one day a week, will help rekindle a slow agni (see page 46 on detoxification).

• Pranayama (yogic breathing exercises) is credited with boosting metabolism and unblocking your channels, shifting stagnant energy, and making you feel more alive. Even sitting still or lying down and breathing deeply from your stomach for 5 minutes will help.

Change is important to the stable kapha; shake off old habits and challenge yourself with new activities. Take positive action and open up to new experiences, adding some adventure, meet new people, seek variety, take a risk, and add spontaneity into your life. Free yourself of all the "stuff" you are accumulating and holding on to, the emotional baggage, and objects you are sentimentally attached to. Travel as frequently as possible and enjoy life to its fullest.

# Menu Plan for Kapha

## Monday
Bliss breakfast drink, page **68** (if you are hungry midmorning, snack on a piece of fruit)
Mom's chicken stew, page **71**, with a little rye bread
Cannellini beans with kale, page **134**, with salt and pepper herb polenta, page **140**

## Tuesday
Egg-white scrambled eggs with a slice of toasted rye bread
Lightly spiced smoked trout tortilla, page **102**, with vegetables/salad on the side
Vegetables and edamame in chile, ginger coconut broth, page **122**, with cellophane noodles

## Wednesday
Quinoa and sweet spice oatmeal, page **63**
Broiled tofu, green bean, noodle, and sesame salad, page **90**
Ayurvedic lentil curry, page **128**, with savoy cabbage with peas, page **133**, served with spinach and onion flat bread, page **141**, or some quinoa or millet

## Thursday
Rye bread, plain or spread with a little honey
Hearty Puy lentil and herb soup, page **72**, with some rice stirred in or on the side
Hianese chicken rice, page **118**, and a vegetable from your list

## Friday
Spiced fruit compote, page **67**
Warm eggplant, quinoa, and tofu salad with ginger dressing, page **83**
Cornmeal-crusted chicken, page **113**, with sautéed corn with peppers, page **132**

## Saturday
Lemon and blueberry cornmeal pancakes, page **60**
Lentil and rice oatmeal (khicheri), page **52** (to give your system a break)
Star anise and ginger steamed fish, page **100**, on a bed of sprouting broccoli
Baked spice-stuffed apple, page **147**

## Sunday
Spicy scrambled tofu with rye bread, page **64**
Snack on crudités or air-popped corn or carrot sticks with a little hummus, page **87**, if hungry
Red onion, radicchio, and goat cheese pizza, page **131**, with some greens on the side

Here is a general menu to give you an idea of a week's worth of meals. This is just a guide, you can vary it as much as you like, there are more recipes to choose from and there are food charts on pages 153–158 to help you make up your own meals. If you have an easy working arrangement, definitely make lunch your main meal and eat a light dinner. Begin your day with hot water and lemon. Breakfast can be skipped if you are not hungry or have some fresh fruit from your list. The spiced fruit compote is probably the best breakfast for you.

## Kapha pantry basics
Rye bread, buckwheat (soba) noodles, glass/cellophane noodles, pearl barley, firm and soft tofu, dried beans and lentils, dried shiitake mushrooms, cornmeal, corn or flour tortillas, honey, quinoa, millet, spices.

# Ayurveda and Weight Loss

We live in ironic times—half the world population is, unfortunately, malnourished, the other half is voluntarily so through dieting or bad food choices. As a society, we obsess on the subjects of weight and fat but seem to make little progress toward a healthier attitude to either.

Vata body types are usually thin and light, but often turn to sugary carbohydrates to calm their nerves. These refined products can soon translate into body fat (often around the waist). Also, they have erratic digestive systems, so often have a high level of ama which clogs the system and can lead to weight gain and water retention. If you are vata and have put on weight, identify why. If it is because you turn to calming sweetness when stressed, try a vata-balancing diet to calm your nerves and you should lose weight. If it is your digestive system that seems sluggish, try the ama-reducing diet. If it is neither, follow the weight loss advice on pages 44–45.

Pitta people are lucky in this regard, as they rarely put on weight. If they have a prolonged imbalance, it is possible that they burn out their agni and weaken their digestive system but this is rare. If it does happen, follow a pitta-balancing diet.

Kapha people have a tendency to gain weight and are often the ones who are overweight as they have naturally slow metabolisms, and when imbalanced they often use food as an emotional crutch and can become addicted to eating.

You can also put on weight if taking medicine (many strong medicines are thought to depress agni). Hormonal imbalances or psychological factors such as depression and stress can lead to weight gain. A weakened agni will affect weight and this happens naturally as we age, so we need to adjust our eating habits accordingly.

## My Weight-Loss Story

I was born a chubby baby and grew into an overweight adult. Although I was mostly healthy, strong, and happy, I realized I needed to lose weight and started dieting in my teens. I followed the latest fad diets and, as I am quite disciplined, I always lost weight, but the results were superficial and the pounds returned. Realizing that fad diets were not the answer (erratic eating weakens agni), I decided only to eat foods which were healthy for my body (as far as I knew at the time). I devised a healthy eating plan and started to exercise properly. Healthy eating and living became my mantra and the word "diet" was banished.

My new eating regime consisted of three healthy, low-fat meals a day. I had no refined sugar or bread and switched to brown rice. Breakfast was whole grain cereal with skim milk; lunch, my favorite meal, was anything from Indian food to pasta to a dressed baked potato and salad. If hungry in between meals, I would snack only on fruit. My dinner was always early and light and generally vegetables, salads, or soups with a crunchy apple to follow. I didn't eat dessert and alcohol became something only to sip on the weekends. It worked and I lost 88 pounds.

That was ten years ago and apart from relaxing my tight control over the amount of fat in my food (it is so vital to health) and enjoying a little dessert and drink when I am in the mood, I still eat the same way. Looking back, my diet was typical of a kapha-balancing diet.

# The Healthy Way to Lose Weight

The weight-loss guidelines on the facing page are for losing weight (but read the dosha notes on page 40 first to make sure this is the right course for you). The tips may seem entirely familiar because, on the whole, they correlate with our modern understanding of weight loss. Weight gain is synonymous with kapha as you are adding these qualities to your body, so I would advise you to go on a kapha-balancing diet (see page 38) until you lose the weight. New habits take around three weeks to settle in, so stick with it and give yourself a chance; it gets easier and soon becomes routine. I refer a lot to ama here (see page 14) as a build up of these toxins can lead to weight gain.

New eating habits take about three weeks
to settle in, so stick with it and this new way
of eating will soon become easier.

- Start your day with a cup of hot water with lemon slices to cleanse the metabolic tract. If you wish, you can add a little honey to the water once it has cooled a little.

- Barley water is another great weight-loss drink. Boil a handful of pearl or pot barley in 8 cups of water until soft. Drain (reserving the water) and flavor the barley water with lemon and honey to taste and drink. It reduces fat and relieves swelling and water retention. (Eat the grains in your meal.)

- Drink hot water throughout the day as this strengthens digestion and stops you eating when you only think you are hungry but are thirsty. Sip warm or room temperature water with meals.

- Make lunch the biggest meal of the day as your agni is at its strongest at 1pm. As it is quite low at night, dinners should be small, light, and vegetarian. Do not eat again until breakfast. Most of us eat a small, quick lunch at work and a large dinner at home, which can add weight as your metabolism is low, and also ama as your agni is low. If you are able to switch these meals, you will feel much lighter at night, hungry for a proper breakfast, and largely eating more healthily.

- Remember portion control! Eat until you are half full and then stop. Overeating not only leads to weight gain but also an increased appetite and the accumulation of ama.

- Eat a varied diet. Each food and taste has a distinct function in the body. If these functions are not fulfilled, the body will crave more food in order to bridge the gap and we will feel the need to eat more despite the fact that we are not hungry. Make each meal count!

- Eat freshly cooked meals as much as possible. Leftovers have lost much of their vitality and nutrition. As you reheat them, they will continue to deteriorate in this way and you often end up eating empty calories and can crave more, see above.

- Your diet should be dominated by vegetables with moderate amounts of grains and protein. Dessert should be a treat and is best shared with a friend. I need to enjoy my meals so I cook all my favorite dishes but with less fat and eat smaller portions of the fun bits and add bulk with vegetables.

- Make sure your agni is healthy, and keep it strong (see page 14). If you are kapha body type, doing a liquid fast (see page 46) once a week is very beneficial for your agni.

- Avoid heavy foods and dairy products, lots of fat, and red meat (Ayurveda actually advises a vegetarian diet as all meat is heavy when compared to vegetable-based proteins).

- Eat your meals or snack only when you are hungry. Plan what to eat before you actually become hungry so that you do not turn to something you later wished you hadn't.

- Exercise regularly to a moderate intensity and try to stay active throughout the day. Exercise is a cure for almost everything, it keeps us mentally and physically agile, strengthens our agni, keeps our weight in check, and is good for our bones and muscles.

- Reduce the amount of stress in your life as this can make you gain weight, either by sending you to the nearest cookie jar or by depressing your agni. Practicing yoga and meditation will help control the emotions that lead us to binge or stress.

- Do not fall asleep straight after eating—be active (but do not exercise either).

- Pranayama (yogic breathing exercise) helps to control the emotional issues, stress, and cravings that can lead to weight gain.

# The Ayurveda Detox

Anything harmful or not useful to the body is considered a toxin, whether it comes from pollutants, chemicals, additives, or from within your own body as ama. Ama is formed when any food is not digested properly and is considered to be the root of all disease. It is believed that negative thoughts and emotions and depression all give rise to ama. A toxic buildup is often the reason we feel tired, unwell, have headaches, cellulite, gain weight, and suffer other serious disorders. Unfortunately, it is almost impossible not to accumulate ama in our everyday life, so Ayurvedic doctors advise all adults to undergo regular detox therapies.

Fortunately, it is possible to detox at home. When agni is not working on digesting and assimilating the nutrients from our meals, it is free to burn the toxins in the gut. So, all we need to do is give our digestive system a break so it has a chance to burn ama. This is achieved by fasting, which will burn ama as well as strengthen your agni. A fast should give you energy, clarity of mind, a feeling of lightness, and a really great glow. It is not a diet. The aim is to burn toxins, not fat, but as ama can lead to weight gain, it will help in the long run. I have included three different detox options. Try the intense liquid fast (below), the three-day fast on page 49, or the milder ama-reducing diet on page 50.

## The hard-core liquid fast

This is an intense 1 to 2 day fast to be done once a week, fortnightly, or a month. It is an all-liquid fast where you eat only light vegetable soups and juices. The sweet taste increases ama so if you crave a fruit juice or a sweet vegetable juice (e.g. carrot juice), dilute it with a little water. Start the day with a cup of hot water and lemon (you can add honey, which has detoxifying properties, but only after 5 minutes of it cooling). Drink the Detox Tea (see page 51) or hot water throughout the day. Don't do this fast if you are young, old, weak, ill, or have a vata imbalance.

For a detox to be effective, we should try to rest the mind along with the digestive system, as these two activities demand the most energy from our bodies. We need to try to stay calm and not be overactive, so that the body has energy to work on the toxins.

# Detoxifying Green Mung Bean Soup

## The strong three-day fast

Eat a bowl of this detoxifying soup with some simple steamed or sautéed green leafy vegetables (with an edge of bitterness, ideally) for breakfast, lunch, and dinner for 3 to 5 consecutive days. Only eat when there is genuine hunger and the previous meal has been digested. You will be nourished but will burn lots of ama.

**Makes 2 to 3 bowls**

**The basic soup**
½ cup green mung beans, washed in
     several changes of water
½ teaspoon ground turmeric
4 cups water
¼ teaspoon asafetida
Pinch of freshly ground black pepper
     (vata and kapha only)
Rock salt to taste
1 rounded tablespoon chopped
     cilantro

**Basic tarka (flavored oil)**
¾ teaspoon cumin seeds
¾ teaspoon ground coriander

**Kapha-balancing ingredients**
¾ teaspoon ghee
1 teaspoon minced ginger
¼ teaspoon garam masala

**Pitta-balancing ingredients**
1½ teaspoons ghee
⅓ teaspoon ground fennel or to taste

**Vata-balancing ingredients**
2 teaspoons ghee
1 teaspoon minced ginger
¼ teaspoon garam masala or to taste
¾ teaspoon lemon juice

This is the soup that Rebecca Kriese (a wonderful Ayurvedic practitioner who has helped guide me) recommends for detoxifying and revitalizing the body. It is very effective for removing toxins and stagnated foods from the body, and is ideal for kindling the digestive fire, reducing swelling and water retention, and cleansing the liver, gallbladder, and vascular system. It helps you to lose weight and relieves digestive problems, bloating, and body ache. The green mung is preferable to the yellow split mung, as the outer green skin is rich in minerals and has a cleansing action on the digestive tract.

Wash the mung beans thoroughly and then soak them either overnight or for at least 4 hours before cooking. Bring the lentils and the fresh water to a gentle simmer, add the turmeric, and simmer for 30 to 40 minutes, or until soft, adding more water if necessary.

Once the beans are cooked, heat the ghee in your smallest saucepan, add the asafetida, and let sizzle for 5 seconds. Add the cumin seeds and ginger (if using) and cook for 30 seconds until the seeds have darkened and become aromatic. Add the remaining spices, let them sizzle for 20 seconds, and then stir them into your soup. Let the soup simmer for another 2 minutes, add rock salt to taste, and then serve warm with cilantro leaves and lemon juice (if you are vata).

**Variations**
Add some vegetables such as spinach (and nutmeg), other greens, or grated carrots to the blended soup and cook until done to your liking. Add a little coconut milk for a different flavor (not for detox).

# The milder ama-reducing diet

This is a gentler one- or two-week fast where you eat small portions of easy-to-digest meals. Everything must be organic, natural, and unrefined. Start your mornings where possible with hot water and lemon (add honey if you like after it has cooled for 5 minutes).

• Meals should all be freshly and lightly cooked; no processed, canned, or refined foods.

• Eat your main meal at lunchtime when your digestion is strongest. Make sure your dinner is light and eaten early enough to be digested before you sleep.

• Do not overeat; even eating too much of anything will overburden your digestive system and produce ama.

• Do not snack between meals unless you are genuinely hungry.

• Steam or sauté vegetables with a few spices and ginger. Include lots of leafy greens and bitter vegetables. Avoid potatoes, sweet potatoes, cabbage, mushrooms, eggplants, tomatoes, and Brussels sprouts. Light vegetable soups are great. Sprouted mung beans are said to have good detoxifying properties (cook before eating).

• Avoid salads and raw vegetables unless they are juiced.

• Limit fruits to those that are not too sweet and dense —apples, grapes, and pomegranates all have detoxifying properties. Fruit juices should be diluted with water.

• Include rice, barley, millet, quinoa, and rye in your diet, but avoid wheat as much as possible. White rice is particularly easy to digest and khicheri, a creamy rice and lentil dish (see page 52), is the quintessential detox meal.

• For protein, include lots of mung and red lentils; avoid all meats and eggs. Include a little tofu if you know you can digest it.

• Avoid all dairy with the exception of lassi, a sweet or spiced savory drink, which is nutritious, light on the system, and aids digestion (see page 152).

• Avoid nuts, although a few seeds are fine (ideally ground).

• Cook with little fat, some of which can be ghee as it strengthens agni.

• Avoid all sugars (dessert, cookies, refined sugar, etc.); honey is okay in moderation.

• Avoid all alcohol, canned, carbonated, and ice-cold drinks, coffee, and tea.

• Avoid ketchup, mayo, soy. sauce, salad creams, and tamarind.

• Cook with ginger, cardamom, fennel seeds, black pepper, ajowan seeds, and nutmeg as they aid digestion.

• Drink detox tea or hot water throughout the day.

Exercise regularly but moderately and according to your body type (see the individual doshas section) to stimulate digestion and help eliminate toxins. Sunbathing (using sunscreen), sauna, and steam help flush toxins out of the system. After the fast, introduce normal eating slowly and try not to go back to old, ama-producing eating habits.

Detoxification is taken very seriously in Ayurveda and if you are worried about an illness rather than simply wanting to cleanse your system, you should consult an Ayurvedic doctor for a deeper treatment.

For the detox to be effective, we should try to rest the mind along with the digestive system as these two activities demand the most energy from our bodies. We need to try to stay calm and not be overactive, so that the body has energy to work on the toxins.

# Detoxifying Tea

Drink throughout the day

4 cups water
¾ teaspoon cumin seeds
1 teaspoon coriander seeds
1 teaspoon fennel seeds
2 ginger slices
½ teaspoon black peppercorns
3 cloves
1 cinnamon shard

Boil all the ingredients together for 5 to 7 minutes and let seep for another 5 minutes. Strain the spices and pour into a teapot or thermos. (Also great steeped in a little water and mixed with pomegranate juice or apple juice.)

### PITTA
Pitta should omit the peppercorns and reduce the amount of cloves and ginger. Add a sprig of mint.

# Khicheri

**Serves 1, can be doubled**

**Base**
Scant ¼ cup basmati rice, washed well
⅛ cup yellow mung lentils, washed well
⅛ teaspoon ground turmeric
1¾ cups water

**Basic tarka (flavored oil)**
1 teaspoon ghee
Pinch of asafetida
½ teaspoon cumin seeds
Salt to taste

This rice and lentil oatmeal is the ultimate Ayurvedic dish. It is simple, nourishing, well-balanced, and well-cooked so is easy on the digestive system, which can then work on burning up toxins instead. I often eat it when I have been feeling a little sluggish. Some people doing a long detox often live off khicheri. It is great for all doshas although you can tailor it to your own dosha (see below). It is always made with ghee which makes the meal easier to digest (than oil) so I would stick with it and it adds a wonderful buttery flavor, too.

Place all the ingredients for the oatmeal in a saucepan, gently bring to a boil, then simmer, partially covered, for 30 minutes, or until soft. Remove any scum that forms on the surface. You may need to add an extra splash of water if the pan looks too dry.

Heat the ghee in a small saucepan, add the asafetida, and let it sizzle for at least 5 seconds. Add the cumin and cook for 20 seconds, or until it has darkened and is aromatic. Pour into the oatmeal and season to taste.

### VATA
Add vegetables from your list to the oatmeal as above. Follow the tarka for kapha but use 2 good teaspoons of ghee.

### PITTA
Add the same vegetables as kapha (or see the charts on pages 153–158). Keep the tarka simple, although you can use 1½ to 2 teaspoons of ghee.

### KAPHA
Add some vegetables from your list, e.g. a handful of cauliflower florets and a small handful of peas, after 25 minutes of cooking the oatmeal. For the tarka, add 1 tablespoon chopped onion into the oil once the cumin seeds have become aromatic. When the onion is soft, add ½ teaspoon each minced ginger and garlic, and cook gently for 1 minute. Stir into the oatmeal, season with salt and pepper and a pinch of garam masala.

# RECIPES

A healthy Ayurvedic diet was traditionally centered around Indian food but as even I would get bored on a diet of solely Indian food, I have gone further afield for inspiration. This collection of recipes is as varied in taste as in ingredients, so you can cook from the book and eat a healthy diet without getting tired of the same tastes. Although some recipes will be better for you than others, all natural food will nourish you in some way, but it will also affect your doshas. As long as you are aware of this affect (and are not suffering from a serious imbalance) you can balance any meal with the food that you eat the rest of the day. On the whole, try to stick with recipes that will balance your own dosha and that you know you are able to digest.

# Before You Start

Foods work in subtle ways in the body and definitely add up to more than the sum of their parts (protein, fats, calories, etc.). Here are a few ingredients I wanted to highlight as Ayurveda has some really interesting views on them and in some cases, modern nutritionists are starting to agree.

## Ghee

A certain amount of fat is vital to good health, both physically and mentally. But not all fats are created equal and one of the fats labeled "bad" in the West is ghee. Ghee is butter that has been clarified of all milk solids and is one of Ayurveda's prized ingredients. Ayurveda believes food cooked in ghee is easier to digest (compared to food cooked in oil), is cooling (oil is heating), and strengthens agni. It balances pitta and vata (oil only balances vata), is strengthening and nourishing and increases our longevity.

Research has found that ghee has antioxidant, antiviral, and anticarcinogenic properties and is rich in vitamins and minerals. It stimulates secretions of stomach acids which aid digestion and the saturated content of ghee is mainly made up of short-chain fatty acids which are easier to digest than the longer chains present in many oils. One of its components —conjugated linolenic acid—is even thought to help reduce body fat. Ghee has a high burning point so does not produce free radicals in cooking. Include a spoon or two of ghee in your cooking instead of oil to reap some of these benefits.

## Animal protein

Ayurveda is wary of the consumption of animal protein as food for most people, although it was used medicinally for those who were undernourished. Meat is nourishing, strengthening, and heating, but it is quite hard to digest. It was largely avoided by Indians because they believed that killing another being can have a negative impact on their spiritual development. Eating too much meat can also cause lethargy and dullness (see page 21). Even modern scientists believe that eating too much meat is the root of many life-threatening diseases.

From a dosha point of view, animal proteins are sweet, heavy, and heating. In kapha body types, eating too much meat will add heaviness and as kapha do not require the extra nutrition, they do not really need it. When they do eat it, stick to light, white meats. Pitta is aggravated by the heating and heavy properties of meat. Some meats are worse than others—red meats, pork, and shellfish are the most heating so have been left out of this book; fish and chicken are comparatively less heating and are the best options for nonvegetarians. Those with a vata imbalance generally benefit from eating meat as it is known to restore their health, but some meats can be hard to digest so make sure you are able to do so or eat small portions. Choose free-range organic meat or meat from wild animals. I know it is hard to change old habits but it is definitely worth substituting some meats with vegetarian proteins.

Dairy and animal proteins do not combine well in the stomach so you won't see any cream or cheese in any of the fish or chicken recipes.

## Milk

Ayurveda believed raw milk was a fantastic, nourishing food. Traditionally in India, and even in many regions today, milk is delivered raw and then boiled at home to kill off the bacteria. The qualities of milk are sweet, cool, heavy, but many modern Ayurvedic doctors agree that pasteurizing milk changes its energies, making it harder to digest. Milk is best taken alone and separate from salty and sour meals, although it can be cooked with grains into a sweet dish.

The best way of drinking milk is to boil it with a few sweet spices such as cardamom, cinnamon, and nutmeg which balance the cool and heavy nature of milk (sweeten to taste). In this guise, it is thought to increase ojas, our immunity and vitality. Warmed, it is a wonderful food for vata particularly, calming and grounding them. It is also cooling for pitta, but in kaphas it can cause congestion and mucus. Kapha should stick to goat's milk as it is lighter or try rice or soy milk. If your digestive fire is feeling weak, or you are suffering with cough, cold, sinuses, or mucus, milk is best avoided until the symptoms have cleared.

## Yogurt

Yogurt is deceptive as the sourness will heat rather than cool the body. It will increase kapha with its heaviness and pitta with its sourness. Yogurt can clog body channels, blocking the flow of vata and causing stagnation and water retention. It also has a dampening quality so lowers the intensity of agni. It is best taken at lunchtime when agni is at its highest or diluted and drunk as a lassi (see page 152) which delivers the nutrients of yogurt and is easy to digest. Avoid combining with meats, fruits, and even other dairy products.

## Fruit

Ayurveda believes ripe fruits eaten in season are nectar for the body. They are cleansing and increase ojas, the "happy" energy in our body. But fresh fruits are best eaten alone at breakfast or as a snack; they do not combine well with other foods. Cooked and dried fruits go better with meals than fresh fruit.

## Tomatoes

Many Ayurvedic doctors advise patients to steer away from tomatoes. Raw tomatoes can be hard to digest and the skin and seeds are quite indigestible. Even cooked tomatoes should mostly be avoided by pitta as they are sour, and also limited by kapha and vata.

Most of the evidence is undocumented but many Ayurvedic doctors find that tomatoes can increase stiffness and pain in the joints, are heating and damp in the gut, and cause bloating and acidity. In fact, all the vegetables from the nightshade family are viewed with some caution and are always cooked with spices to help agni better digest them. I have included tomatoes in only a few recipes. See how you feel after eating them; if they don't suit you, substitute, where possible, with lemon juice or spices like dried mango or pomegranate powder.

## Wheat

According to Ayurveda, wheat is a fantastic grain; it is sweet, cold, and astringent and was traditionally considered strengthening and nourishing. However, modern-day wheat has a higher gluten content which makes it more sticky, mucoid, and congesting in our system. Gluten can aggravate arthritis, cause allergies, clog channels, and can make you sluggish.

Avoid eating too many refined wheat products and breads. I often use spelt flour, a variety of wheat with a lower gluten content (I substitute like for like). Kamut is another wheat grain with a low gluten content. Include other grains such as barley, quinoa, buckwheat, millet, and cornmeal in your diet.

## Cooking beans

Apart from mung beans, all dried beans need to be soaked before cooking to render them digestible. Soaking them (and even lentils) also reduces cooking time. Wash beans well, checking for any stones. Soak in plenty of water overnight or for 4 to 6 hours. Once soaked, cook in plenty of simmering water (I like to use fresh water) until soft—this can take anywhere from 40 minutes for mung beans to 1¾ hours for chickpeas and kidney beans. To calculate the quantity of beans to soak, divide the given cooked amount by 2.5 (so 3½ ounces/⅝ cup cooked equals 1½ ounces/¼ cup dried).

# BREAKFAST

Breakfast is my favorite meal so I never understand how some people go without. However, Ayurveda is clear that if you are not hungry, you shouldn't eat. Wait until you are hungry, then have something light so that you can still eat your lunch at the proper time.

Vata is kept in balance with warm, cooked food like oatmeal, eggs, or fresh pancakes. Avoid dry cereal, or soften it in room-temperature milk. Instead of coffee, try any milky, spiced masala tea (see page 152).

Pitta should opt for cooling food, such as muesli, granola, cereal, or toast. Avoid salty, fatty breakfasts such as sausages (heating and heavy) as they increase pitta. Stick to egg whites as the yolks are heating. Avoid coffee, tea, orange juice, and yogurt —try a grain milk or fennel and mint tea.

Kapha should only eat if hungry as many are not peckish in the morning. Choose warm, light foods like spiced fruit compote (see page 68). Fruit is best eaten by itself in the morning as it increases immunity and vitality. Warm stewed apples are one of the healthiest ways to start the day for all body types.

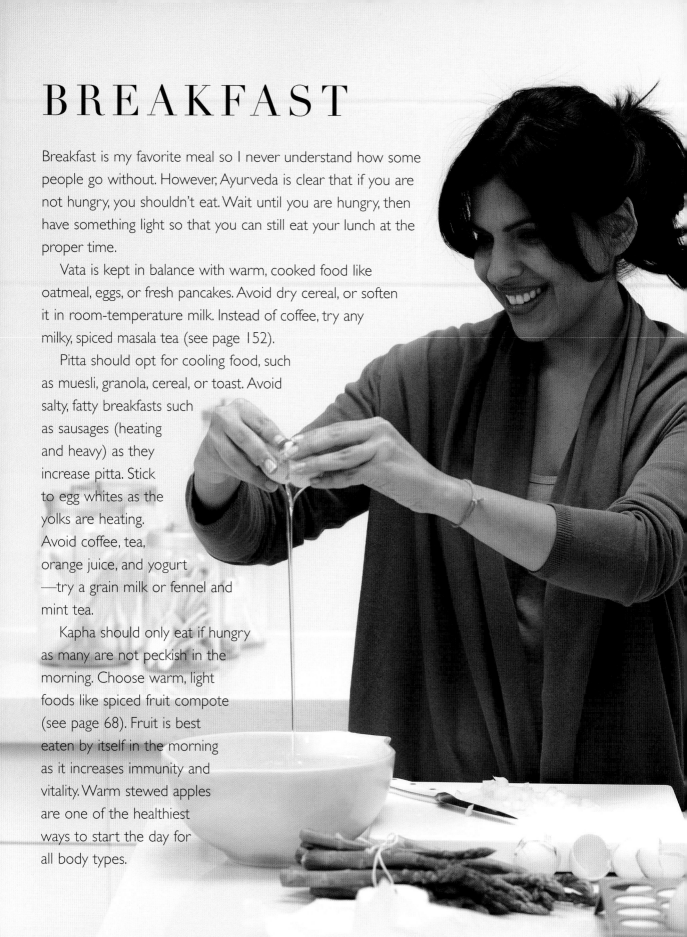

# Cardamom-Laced Semolina

VATA
Ideal for vata

PITTA
A great winter
breakfast

KAPHA
For when you are
extra hungry

This is a wonderful breakfast—warm, easy to digest, and unctuous, but not heavy. It is based on an Indian dessert but the fat and sugar have been reduced to make a healthy grain-based breakfast. It is ideal vata fare, but it is also good for pitta to eat, especially in the colder months. Kapha should ideally have a lighter, nonwheat breakfast, but when you are hungry (many kaphas are not hungry in the morning) make this breakfast with rice or soy milk, add some raisins, reduce the amount of sugar, and drizzle over a little honey. The almonds will need to be soaked overnight.

**Serves 1**

1 teaspoon ghee or butter
   (kapha should use ½ teaspoon)
Scant ¼ to ¼ cup semolina
   (depends how hungry you are)
¾ to generous ¾ cup half milk, half
   water (⅔ cup for a thicker, drier
   dish; generous ¾ cup for an
   oatmeal-like consistency)
1½ to 2 teaspoons sugar
1 green cardamom pod, husk removed
   and seeds pounded in a mortar and
   pestle
3 almonds, soaked overnight in water,
   skinned, and slivered (in winter, try
   toasted sesame seeds)
Honey (kapha) or maple syrup (vata
   and pitta) to drizzle over

Heat the ghee in a small saucepan. Add the semolina and roast for 2 to 3 minutes over medium heat, stirring constantly, until the semolina resembles medium-colored sand. Immediately add the liquid—it will bubble up for a second and then settle down.

Add the sugar and spice and keep stirring for another 2 to 3 minutes, or until the semolina is cooked. It will thicken as it cools, but you can add extra liquid at any time if you prefer a thinner consistency (I like mine quite thick).

Pour into a bowl and serve with almonds or toasted sesame seeds and drizzled with a little honey (kapha) or maple syrup (vata and pitta).

# Lemon and Blueberry Cornmeal Pancakes

VATA
Use oats instead of
cornmeal—see method

PITTA
Use oats instead of
cornmeal—see method

KAPHA
Cornmeal is great
for kapha

These versatile pancakes are wonderful breakfast or brunch fare and take minutes to cook from start to finish. They are egg-free so are good for vegetarians, and light and fluffy but with the slight crunch of cornmeal, which is drying and therefore a better grain for kapha than wheat. You can also add oats instead of the cornmeal for vata or pitta, see below.

**Makes 12 small pancakes,
can be halved**

2 teaspoons butter
⅓ cup all-purpose (or spelt) flour
⅓ cup cornmeal
1¾ tablespoons raw cane sugar
1 teaspoon baking powder
½ teaspoon lemon zest
1 rounded tablespoon dried blueberries
　　or raisins
Generous ½ to scant ⅝ cup (or half
　　yogurt, half water)
1 teaspoon lemon juice
Honey (kapha) or maple syrup (pitta
　　or vata) to drizzle

Melt the butter in a nonstick skillet or pancake pan.

In a bowl, whisk together all the dried ingredients. Make a well in the middle and pour in the buttermilk, lemon juice, and the melted butter. Whisk together from the middle, drawing in the dry ingredients from the side, to make a batter. (For vata and pitta, make the pancakes with scant ½ cup flour and ½ cup quick-cooking oats and use scant ⅔ cup buttermilk.)

Reheat the skillet (you shouldn't need to add any more oil). Add dessert-spoonfuls of the batter to the skillet (one spoonful per pancake), but space them well apart as each pancake will spread to become about 2 inches in diameter—you can probably fit five or six in a large skillet. Turn the heat down a little and cook, undisturbed, until the pancakes start to look set at the base, around 1 minute. Carefully flip them over; the undersides should be golden. Cook on this side for another minute or until the bases are golden too. Place on a plate, cover, and keep warm. Repeat with the remaining batter.

Serve drizzled with honey if you are kapha or maple syrup if you are pitta or vata (who can also add a little butter/ghee to theirs, too).

# Vitality Oatmeal

VATA
Nourishing and
easy to digest

PITTA
Great in winter; can
add dried fruit

KAPHA
Eat only occasionally;
can add dried fruit

**Serves 1**

Scant ½ to generous
  ½ cup rolled oats
1 to 1¼ cups milk, water,
  or a mixture of both
  (I use half soy milk and
  half water)
1 piece of broken star
  anise, optional
⅓ to ½ teaspoon ground
  cinnamon
½ teaspoon vanilla extract,
  optional
Sweetener, such as agave
  nectar, maple syrup,
  raw cane sugar, or
  honey to taste
1 tablespoon pumpkin
  seeds, ground flaxseeds,
  or pistachios

In the West oatmeal is a standard breakfast, enjoyed for the heart-healthy properties of oats. From an Ayurvedic point of view, it is a warming, nourishing breakfast that is easy on the stomach. When you bring milk to a boil and add a spice, you make it easier to digest, although if your system is feeling a little sluggish, it would be better to choose a grain milk, such as rice, soy, or almond milk, or cook with plain water. It is hard to determine quantities here—you should eat until you feel half full. I am hungry in the mornings and I cook about a ½ cup, but see how you feel and adjust the quantities accordingly.

Bring the oats, milk, water, and star anise (if using) to a boil in a small saucepan. Simmer until the oats are soft—mine take about 5 to 6 minutes but other brands might take longer. Add a little more liquid if necessary.

Stir in the cinnamon, vanilla extract, and seeds or nuts, sweeten to taste, and serve.

**Opposite:** Quinoa and Sweet Spice Oatmeal (foreground) and Vitality Oatmeal

# Quinoa and Sweet Spice Oatmeal

VATA
Omit the dried
fruit

PITTA
A good breakfast

KAPHA
A good breakfast

**Serves 1 generously**

¼ cup quinoa, well-rinsed
¾ cup milk of your choice
  (rice milk, almond milk,
  soy milk, or cow's milk)
¾ cup water
2 teaspoons dried
  blueberries (pitta), dried
  cranberries, or raisins
⅓ teaspoon ground
  cinnamon
½ star anise (optional)
½ teaspoon vanilla extract
½ teaspoon orange zest
Sweetener, such as maple
  syrup, or honey to taste
1 to 2 teaspoons pumpkin
  seeds

Quinoa is a grain full of amino acids. It is a complete protein so makes a wonderful breakfast, warm in the winter or cold in the summer. A good breakfast for all doshas (vata should omit the dried fruit) and great if your system is feeling sluggish as it is a very light grain. It doesn't have the creamy flavor of oats, so add other tasty ingredients. There are no rules—you can change the flavorings as you like.

Put the quinoa, milk, and water in a small pan. Bring to a boil, partially cover, and cook for 30 minutes, or until the quinoa is just soft. After 15 minutes add the dried fruit, spices, vanilla extract, and orange zest. If the pan looks dry, add a splash of warm water. Once the quinoa is soft, adjust consistency to your liking by evaporating excess liquid over high heat or adding a splash of warm water. Sweeten to taste (if adding honey, do so off the heat and do not cook). Sprinkle with the pumpkin seeds.

**Soy milk**
This dish works really well with soy milk but the quinoa should be cooked in water for the first 20 minutes and the soy milk added at this stage.

# Spicy Scrambled Tofu

VATA
Only for vata if you find
tofu easy to digest

PITTA
Great, but avoid other
heating ingredients that day

KAPHA
Great for kapha; serve
with rye bread

This dish is a great breakfast or brunch dish for kapha body types, as it is warming and nourishing but light. For kapha and pitta, tofu is a better protein than eggs and a great start to a busy day. I eat this dish with a little plain whole wheat toast or as part of a meal with flat breads (it goes really well with the Spinach and Onion Flat Breads on page 141, shown here in the photo). This dish is good for vata body types if they find it easy to digest tofu (not all do).

**Serves 1**

1 teaspoon ghee or vegetable oil
1 green chile, pierced with the tip of
    a knife, optional
½ small onion, minced (3 tablespoons)
½ small garlic clove, chopped
½ medium tomato, chopped
½ teaspoon garam masala
½ teaspoon ground cumin
⅛ teaspoon ground turmeric
Salt and freshly ground black pepper
3¾ cups ounces firm tofu, chopped into
    small pieces
Small handful of cilantro leaves,
    chopped

Heat the ghee or oil in a small nonstick skillet. Add the chile and onion and sauté until golden at the edges. Add the garlic and cook for 30 to 40 seconds. Add the tomato, spices, and seasoning and cook over medium heat for 3 to 4 minutes, or until the tomatoes have softened.

Add the tofu and a splash of warm water, then cook for 5 minutes, breaking up and squashing the pieces so the tofu resembles scrambled eggs (I use the back of my wooden spoon, but a potato masher would probably be quicker). Sprinkle over the cilantro and serve hot.

# Asparagus and Goat Cheese Frittata

Eggs are fantastic breakfast or brunch food for vata as they are warming and nourishing but lighter on the system than other types of protein. A frittata is a great way of using up vegetables that are lying around—you can use whatever you have to hand. I love the addition of goat cheese, but the frittata tastes just as good without it. Ideally make this in a small omelet pan or pancake pan so that the frittata is quite deep.

**Serves 2**

3 large asparagus spears, woody ends discarded, sliced thinly on the diagonal
4 large eggs
½ teaspoon salt and a good pinch of freshly ground black pepper
½ teaspoon lemon zest
8 large mint leaves, shredded
1½ teaspoons vegetable oil
1½ teaspoons butter or ghee
½ small to medium onion, chopped
1½ ounces crumbly goat cheese

Blanch the asparagus in a bowl of boiling water for 1 to 2 minutes, or until cooked to your liking, then drain. Whisk the eggs with the seasoning, lemon zest, and mint.

Preheat the broiler to 350°F or medium.

Heat the oil and butter or ghee in a small nonstick omelet or pancake pan (mine is 6 inches in diameter) with a heatproof handle. Add the onion, cook until soft and turning golden at the edges. Add the asparagus, whisked eggs, and goat cheese to the pan. Turn the heat down as low as possible, cover, and cook for 2 to 4 minutes. Uncover and cook until the frittata feels firm about three-quarters the way up.

Remove the pan from the stove and place under the broiler. Broil until the top is lightly browned and has puffed up.

**Variation**
To serve one, halve the quantities and scramble the egg once the onions are done. Serve with whole grain toast.

# Spiced Fruit Compote

**VATA**
See below for extra ingredients

**PITTA**
See below for extra ingredients

**KAPHA**
An ideal breakfast; can add dried fruit

**Serves 1 generously**

⅓ teaspoon cornstarch
3 tablespoons water
1 small apple, cored, cubed or sliced
3 dried prunes
1 cinnamon stick
1 slice of ginger
½ to 1 teaspoon lemon juice or to taste
1 small pear, cored and cubed
½ teaspoon lemon zest
½ to 1 teaspoon honey, maple syrup, or agave syrup

Apples are considered excellent for balancing kapha—they say those with a kapha imbalance should start every day with stewed apple. In fact, once cooked, they are good for all doshas and help increase ojas (our vitality). Pears are great for balancing hormones and for energy. This dish is perfect for winter or summer mornings. It is especially good for pitta in winter, and they can add some flaked coconut and a little butter or ghee. Vata could add 1 tablespoon ground almonds, some flaked coconut, and a little butter or ghee. Prunes are a great source of fiber and vitamins. How long this dish takes to make will depend on how ripe your fruit is. If your pear is already soft, add it toward the end of the cooking time; if it is hard you can add it in with the apples.

Stir the cornstarch into the water to dissolve, then pour into a small saucepan. Add the apple, prunes, cinnamon, ginger, and lemon juice and zest. Cover and cook on low-medium heat for 5 minutes, or until the apple is softening. Stir in the pear, cover, and cook for another 2 to 4 minutes. Uncover and continue to cook until the fruits are soft and cooked and cradled in thick juices (add a spoonful of warm water if necessary).

Take off the heat, stir in the sweetener to taste, and serve.

# Bliss Breakfast Drink

**VATA**
Suits all doshas

**PITTA**
Suits all doshas

**KAPHA**
Suits all doshas

**Serves 1**

14 whole almonds (use only 8 to 9 if blending with milk or it becomes too rich)
3 medium dates
Few strands of saffron, optional
¾ cup water, or half water, half rice milk (delicious!), or any other milk
Pinch of cardamom powder (made by grinding the seeds of one green cardamom pod)

This drink makes a wonderfully light breakfast if you have had a heavy dinner the night before or if your system is feeling a sluggish. It is light, nourishing, and delicious. Dates (once soaked overnight) are a wonderful fruit for all the three doshas as they strengthen tissue and cleanse blood. When mixed with the soaked almonds, they become something of a health tonic and are said to increase ojas (meaning vitality, feeling of well-being, or bliss energy). If you blend the drink with water, use the extra amount of almonds but if using milk, the smaller quantity will be fine.

Soak the almonds and dates overnight in hot water.

In the morning, drain and peel the almonds. If using the saffron, infuse in 1 tablespoon of hot water for 10 minutes.

Tip the almonds into a blender with the dates and water or milk (if using cow's milk, ideally bring to boiling point and cool before using). Blend, then stir in the saffron water and strands (if using) and the ground cardamom and serve.

# White French Toast with Walnuts

VATA
Warm and nourishing;
can use egg yolks too

PITTA
Great balancing dish

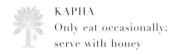

KAPHA
Only eat occasionally;
serve with honey

This is a lighter interpretation of French toast as it is made only with egg white. This is a great pitta-balancing dish as egg whites are neutral and the coconut adds the extra flavor that the egg yolks would usually provide, and it is also cooling on the body. I like to add the jaggery walnuts as I think they work really well with this dish and jaggery is full of great minerals, but you can leave them out or add plain walnuts. This is also a good dish for vata as it is warm, nourishing, and light and for kapha on the odd occasion, but drizzle with honey instead of maple syrup and sprinkle with pumpkin seeds instead of the walnuts.

**Serves 2**

2 egg whites, whisked
1½ teaspoons raw cane sugar
2 slices of medium–thick bread of your choice—I choose whole wheat or spelt
1½ tablespoons dry unsweetened coconut
2 teaspoons vegetable oil
Maple syrup

**Jaggery walnuts** (optional)
¾ ounce jaggery (dark unrefined sugar), grated
2 tablespoons water
12 walnut halves

For the walnuts, add the grated jaggery to a small saucepan with the water. Bring to a simmer and once the jaggery has dissolved, let bubble away for about a minute, or until glossy. Stir in the walnuts and coat well in the sugar. Take out with an oiled spoon and place on an oiled plate. They will cool and firm up in 8 minutes.

Whisk the egg whites with the sugar until well broken up. Pour into a shallow dish and soak the bread in the mixture, then dredge in the coconut so that both sides have a good coating.

Heat the oil in a nonstick skillet. Add the bread and cook over moderate to low heat for 1 to 2 minutes per side until golden and crisp on both sides. Some of the coconut will come off but you can simply sprinkle it over the top of the cooked bread.

Slice on the diagonal and serve drizzled with maple syrup and sprinkled with the walnuts.

# SOUPS

Soups are
a wonderful Ayurvedic
meal option; they are easy to
digest, warming, nourishing, and filling.
They are also a wonderful way of getting
your vegetables. Soups can be nutritious
precursors to a light meal or even a meal
in themselves. This chapter has both.

Soups particularly suit vata as they are warming,
creamy, and easy to digest. If the soup is vegetarian, you
can also stir in a little cream or even Parmesan at the end.
You can make them more substantial by serving with some
fresh bread (try spelt, oat bread, or other whole grain) and little
bit of butter or even some cooked rice stirred in at the end.

Soups are also good for kapha as they are warming, easy to
digest, and filling but not heavy. Avoid bread with the soup but
try some homemade baked tortillas, rice or corn cakes, or rye
bread, or stir in some cooked brown rice or pearl barley to
make it more substantial.

Soups that are not steaming hot are also fine for pitta. Serve
with bread, cooked rice, or barley (as above).

# Mom's Chicken Stew

VATA
Ideal fare for vata, but
opt for thigh meat

PITTA
Serve with buttered
bread if hungry

KAPHA
Great for kapha, but
opt for breast meat

This soup is based on my mother's chicken stew (except that she added a lot of Parmesan at the end). This is quite a retro recipe, but it is such a wholesome dish, which works really with the principles of Ayurveda. This soup is good and nourishing for everybody (vata and kapha can add some freshly ground black pepper to taste). I would eat this soup for lunch or a light dinner as it is, but if you are quite hungry, serve with a little bread (buttered if you are vata or pitta).

**Serves 4 generously**

1½ to 2½ tablespoons olive oil, vegetable oil, or ghee (kapha 1½ tablespoons, vata 2½ tablespoons, pitta 2 tablespoons)
1 bay leaf
3 thyme sprigs
1 large onion, chopped
6 garlic cloves, chopped
1 tablespoon cornstarch
4 cups good-quality chicken stock
3 chicken thighs or 2 large breasts, skinned
1 medium potato, peeled and cut into ½-inch cubes
1 small leek (white parts only), finely sliced
2 medium carrots, sliced into ¾-inch pieces
5 ounces cauliflower, cut into 1-inch florets
3½ ounces fine green beans, halved
2 celery stalks, sliced into ½-inch pieces
Salt
3 tarragon sprigs
Handful of parsley

Heat the oil or ghee in a large nonstick saucepan, add the bay leaf, thyme, and onion, and sauté for 8 to 10 minutes, or until golden. Add the garlic and cook for 30 seconds and follow with cornstarch, stir well to mix, and add the stock and chicken. Bring to a boil, cover, and simmer gently for 10 to 25 minutes (breast should take 10 to 12 minutes and thighs 25 minutes), or until the chicken is cooked all the way through (pierce with a sharp knife and check that the juices run clear).

Remove the chicken from the saucepan, add the potato, leek, carrots, cauliflower, beans, and celery and simmer until soft. Meanwhile, shred or chop the chicken into small pieces.

Take out a ladleful of the vegetables from the saucepan and puree with a little of the soup until smooth, then stir back into the soup with the chicken. Taste, adjust the seasoning, then stir in the tarragon and parsley, and serve.

# Hearty Lentil and Herb Soup

VATA
Garnish with Parmesan

PITTA
Great for pitta

KAPHA
Great for kapha; can add
chile and buckwheat pasta

One-pot meals that cook slowly, allowing all the ingredients to cook together at an easy pace, are the ultimate meals in Ayurveda. This dish is easy to eat and easy to digest. You can add a little pasta to the cooking soup for a more substantial meal (kapha can add buckwheat pasta) or serve with a roll of whole grain (spelt or rye) bread. Vata can finish the dish with a spoon of freshly grated Parmesan.

**Serves 4**

2 to 3 tablespoons olive oil (kapha
    2 tablespoons, pitta 2½ tablespoons,
    vata 3 tablespoons)
2 rosemary sprigs
2 thyme sprigs
1 medium onion, minced
1 carrot, chopped
1 celery stalk, chopped
½ leek, sliced
2 garlic cloves, crushed
1 dried red chile (kapha only)
2¾ cups vegetable stock
Generous 1⅛ cups Puy lentils, washed
Salt and freshly ground black pepper
Small handful of parsley, minced
A squeeze of lemon (optional)

Heat the oil in a large nonstick saucepan. Add the rosemary, thyme, onion, carrot, celery, and leek and sweat, covered, over low heat for 6 to 7 mminutes, or until the onions are soft.

Add the garlic, dried chile (if using), stock, and lentils, bring to a boil, then cover and simmer gently for 25 minutes, or until the lentils are cooked. Pour about one-third of the soup into a blender, puree to a paste, then stir back into the saucepan along with seasoning, parsley, and lemon juice (if using) to taste. Add extra warm water if you prefer a thinner consistency, then serve.

# South Indian Haddock and Corn Chowder

VATA
Serve with buttered
bread

PITTA
Omit the chile

KAPHA
Eat occasionally
as it is cooling

I have always loved chowders—big bowls of creamy, smoky, comforting deliciousness. However, Ayurveda is very vocal about not mixing dairy with animal proteins so I have made this chowder with coconut milk instead and spiced it up a little to complete the Southern Indian touch. This soup is good for vata and pitta (leave out the chile), served with a hunk of bread (buttered if you are vata). It is also light enough to be eaten by those with a kapha imbalance as long as you don't serve it with anything else.

**Serves I generously,
can be doubled**

1 to 2 teaspoons vegetable oil or ghee
(kapha 1 teaspoon, pitta
1½ teaspoons, vata 2 teaspoons)
½ teaspoon mustard seeds
5 curry leaves (optional)
½ small onion, chopped
1 green chile, pierced with the tip of
a knife, optional
⅔ cup coconut milk
⅔ cup water
5 ounces potatoes, peeled and cut into
¾-inch cubes
⅓ cup corn kernels, fresh or frozen
and defrosted
Salt and lots of freshly ground black
pepper
2½ ounces smoked haddock fillet,
skinned
4 ounces unsmoked haddock fillet,
skinned
Large handful of baby or whole leaf
spinach (shredded if whole leaf)

Heat the oil in a small nonstick saucepan. Add the mustard seeds; once they splutter, add the curry leaves, onion, and chile. Cook for 40 seconds, then add the coconut milk and water and bring to a boil. Add the potatoes and fresh corn (if using), bring back to a boil, cover, and cook until the potatoes are soft. Mash a few pieces to help thicken the soup. Add in the frozen corn (if using) and adjust the consistency of the soup, if necessary, by adding a little extra water from the kettle.

Adjust the seasoning, add the fish and spinach, cover, and simmer on low heat for 3 to 4 minutes, or until the fish is cooked and flakes easily.

# Spicy Corn Soup

VATA
Serve with bread

PITTA
Serve with bread and
omit the chile

KAPHA
Serve with baked
tortilla chips

**Serves 4**

1½ teaspoons ghee or 1 tablespoon
   vegetable oil
1½ medium onions, sliced
½-ounce piece ginger, roughly
   chopped
4 garlic cloves, roughly chopped
1 to 2 green chiles, pierced with the
   tip of a knife
½ teaspoon ground turmeric
1½ teaspoons ground cumin
1½ teaspoons ground coriander
½ to 1 teaspoon garam masala
Salt
4 ears corn, corn cut off with
   a serrated knife (one handful
   reserved for garnish, see right)
Handful of cilantro, chopped

This is a wonderful soup which is creamy and delicious, and good for all the doshas (although pitta should leave out the chile). The garnish is optional but does add some great texture to the soup. Serve with baked tortilla chips (see below) for kapha, as it is or with some bread for pitta and vata. Pitta should balance out the spices by avoiding eating heating foods for the rest of the day.

Heat the oil in a large nonstick saucepan. Add the onions and cook until soft and golden brown at the edges. Add the ginger, garlic, and chile and cook, stirring, for 40 seconds. Add all the spices and salt, give the pan a good few second stir, then add all but the reserved handful of corn (if you are making the garnish). Pour in enough water to come 1½ inches above the corn, add the bare cobs for extra flavor, bring to a boil, cover, and simmer for 15 to 20 minutes, or until the corn is tender crisp. Remove the cobs.

Take off the heat and blend into a smooth soup. Pass through a strainer to remove any unprocessed corn skins. Adjust the water content for a creamy soup, adjust seasoning, bring back to a boil, and serve garnished with the chopped cilantro or the corn garnish below.

For optional garnish: add 1 teaspoon oil to a small, nonstick saucepan. Add ½ teaspoon of cumin seeds and once they sizzle, add the reserved corn and half a red bell pepper, chopped. Sauté for 7 to 9 minutes, or until crisp tender. Add the cilantro.

## Baked Tortillas Chips

1 corn tortilla
A pinch of salt and freshly ground black pepper
1 teaspoon vegetable oil

Preheat the oven to 350°F. Rub both sides of the tortilla with the oil, then sprinkle over the salt and pepper. Halve the tortilla, then halve again. Stack the quarters on top of each other and cut into more wedges. Place straight on the oven rack and bake for 7 minutes, or until they are lightly golden. They will firm up as they cool.

# Tridoshic Asparagus Soup

VATA
Suits all doshas

PITTA
Omit pepper and
possibly garam masala

KAPHA
Suits all doshas

**Serves 2**

1½ teaspoons vegetable oil
   or ghee
½ small to medium onion,
   sliced
1 fat garlic clove, chopped
9 ounces asparagus, woody
   ends discarded, sliced
   into ½-inch circles,
   leaving the tips longer
2 ounces potato, peeled
   and cut into cubes
⅔ cup water
⅔ cup vegetable stock
½ teaspoon garam masala
   (omit if you have a
   serious pitta imbalance)
Salt and freshly ground
   black pepper (pitta
   should omit the pepper)

Asparagus is a great vegetable that suits all three doshas. Apart from its many inherent minerals, it is considered very good for fertility. It was also considered an aphrodisiac so was sometimes called "lady with the 100 husbands." As with all Ayurvedic soups, it is made without cream, although vata and, to a lesser extent, pitta can add a little  A great start to a meal or with a little bread for a light meal.

Heat the ghee or oil in a medium nonstick pan. Add the onion and sauté for 4 to 5 minutes, or until soft. Add the chopped garlic and cook for another 30 to 40 seconds, stirring often. Add the asparagus, potatoes, water, and stock. Bring to a boil, then cover and cook gently for 10 minutes, or until the vegetables are just soft.

Puree until smooth. Reheat if necessary, stir in the garam masala, and season to taste with salt and pepper, then serve.

**Opposite:** Tridoshic Asparagus Soup (in pale bowls) and Fennel Vichyssoise with Tarragon (in darker bowls)

# Fennel Vichyssoise with Tarragon

VATA
Suits all doshas

PITTA
Suits all doshas

KAPHA
Use less ghee

**Serves 2 to 3**

½ to 1 tablespoon ghee
   (kapha should
   use ⅓ tablespoon)
1 leek, white parts only,
   sliced
1 large fennel bulb,
   chopped, fronds
   reserved
9 ounces potatoes, peeled
   and cut into small cubes
1 garlic clove, sliced
2½ cups vegetable or
   good-quality chicken
   stock
Salt
⅓ teaspoon fennel seeds,
   ground to a powder
10 tarragon leaves

Soups are normally associated with the winter months, but they are so easy to digest that they should be eaten year round. Here is one that works really well in the summer. Fennel is cooling on the body and helps digest food. Serve as it is as an appetizer or eat as a light meal with a hunk of bread (kapha should stick to rye, buckwheat, or barley flours and vata and pitta should try spelt bread). To make it more special, you can add a little smoked trout on top or swirl in a little cream (pitta and vata only).

Heat the ghee in a large nonstick saucepan. Add the leek and fennel (reserving the fronds) and sauté over medium heat for 5 minutes. Add the potatoes, garlic, and stock. Bring to a boil, then cover and simmer for 15 minutes, or until the vegetables are soft.

Pass through a food mill or blend until smooth. Return to the pan and add a little more water from the kettle, if necessary. Season to taste and stir in the ground fennel seeds and tarragon leaves. Serve garnished with the fennel fronds.

# Carrot and Lentil Soup

VATA
Suits all doshas

PITTA
Suits all doshas

KAPHA
Suits all doshas

**Serves 2 generously**

1½ to 2½ teaspoons ghee or vegetable oil (kapha 1½ teaspoons, pitta 2 teaspoons, vata 2½ teaspoons)
½ medium onion, chopped
¼-ounce piece ginger, roughly chopped
2 small garlic cloves, chopped
1 teaspoon ground coriander
1 teaspoon ground cumin
Salt and lots of freshly ground black pepper
11 ounces carrots, sliced
2 tablespoons red lentils, washed
½ teaspoon vegetable bouillon stock powder, dissolved in 2¾ cups water
Handful of cilantro

A delicious vibrant soup that is sweet but also savory. The lentils give the soup body, protein, and fiber, as well as many minerals. Carrots are a fantastic vegetable and are great for warming up kapha and vata, only warming up pitta slightly so pitta can enjoy this as well, especially when eaten in the cooler months. This is typical of an Ayurvedic soup as it is light and nourishing—the simpler the food, the easier it is to digest. Eat as an appetizer or stir in some cooked rice for a more substantial meal.

Heat the ghee or oil in a small nonstick saucepan. Add the onion and cook gently until golden, then add the ginger and garlic and stir for 40 to 60 seconds. Add the spices and seasoning; stir for 20 seconds. Add the carrots, lentils, and stock. Bring to a boil, then cover and simmer for 20 minutes.

Take off the heat and blend to make a smooth soup. Pour back into the pan and add extra water if the soup is too thick for your liking. Reheat, taste, and adjust seasoning. Serve topped with cilantro.

**Opposite:** Carrot and Lentil Soup, with Simple Rice Pilaf (see page 138)

# Fresh Pea Soup

VATA
Suits all doshas

PITTA
Great for pitta

KAPHA
May want to omit the pesto

**Serves 4**

1 tablespoon ghee or butter
½ teaspoon cumin seeds
1 small to medium onion, finely sliced
3 fat garlic cloves, chopped
5 cups green peas
Salt
1 teaspoon sugar
3½ cups water
2½ tablespoons mint leaves

**Pumpkin seed pesto**
1¼ tablespoons mint leaves
1½ tablespoons extra virgin olive oil
¼ cup pumpkin seeds

This pea soup is light and simple, but vibrant. It is great for all doshas but particularly good for pitta. I don't cook this soup with stock as I feel it would overpower the simple flavors, but you can add it if you wish. The pumpkin seed and mint pesto is wonderful and goes really well with the peas. Those with a strong kapha imbalance may want to leave out the pumpkin seed and mint pesto and simply blend scant ¼ cup of the pumpkin seeds into the soup instead. You can make this soup with defrosted frozen peas. Serve as it is or with some bread.

Heat the ghee or butter in a large nonstick saucepan. Add the cumin seeds and cook gently for 20 seconds. Add the onion and cook until soft, then stir in the garlic and cook, stirring, for 40 seconds. Add the peas, salt, sugar, and water, bring to a boil, and cook, covered, for 10 to 15 minutes, or until the peas are soft.

Add the mint and blend to a smooth soup. Return to the heat, adjust the seasoning, and the consistency, adding a little more water or cooking at high heat for a few minutes to reduce, until the soup is creamy.

For the pesto, pound together the mint and oil until smooth, then coarsely pound the pumpkin seeds into the pesto. Pour the soup into bowls, stir in a spoonful of pesto, and serve.

# SALADS

Salads are the elixir we feel will solve all our weight
issues, but they can be tough on digestive systems
and we are not all able to extract the nutrients.
Salads often have the same qualities as vata (light,
cold, rough) so will increase this dosha, but as
vata may find them hard to digest, eat them at
lunchtime when agni is strongest and in summer
to balance heat. Dress well as the oil will counter the
rough, light qualities, and try warm, cooked salads. Kapha
may also find salads hard to digest and their cold, damp
quality will add to your cool constitution, but as they are also
light and rough, they help balance kapha's heavy, oily qualities.
Again, eat only for a summer lunch—warm salads with
spices are ideal. Pitta often love salads as you crave
cooling foods and your agni should be
strong enough to digest
them. Dress
your salads
with lemon
juice.

# Warm Eggplant, Quinoa, and Tofu Salad with Ginger Dressing

**VATA**
Can substitute chicken for the tofu

**PITTA**
Great for pitta

**KAPHA**
Good for kapha; omit the pine nuts

A delicious salad that I love to eat warm, but it also works cold. Quinoa is a wonderful ancient grain that is gluten-free and easy to digest. It is particularly good for those with a kapha and pitta imbalance. Tofu is a healthy way of eating protein and should be included in all diets (some with a vata imbalance may find it hard to digest, but you can substitute cooked chicken). There are differing opinions on eggplants—like all other vegetables they have a lot of immune-boosting properties and heart-healthy properties, but as a family of the nightshade family, they can aggravate allergies and arthritis so eat in moderation if you are prone to these. Kapha should omit the pine nuts.

**Serves 2**

2 teaspoons vegetable oil
1 medium purple eggplant, sliced
   ½ inch thick and cut into halves
   or quarters
7 ounces tofu, cut into cubes
Generous ¼ cup quinoa, cooked
   according to the package directions
3 handfuls of small lettuce leaves
25 large mint leaves, shredded
1½ tablespoons toasted pine nuts,
   roughly chopped (for pitta and
   vata only)
Salt and freshly ground black pepper

**Dressing**
1½ to 2 tablespoons vegetable oil
2 teaspoons ginger paste (made
   by grating ¼ to ⅓-ounce piece
   ginger on a fine microplane grater)
2 to 3 teaspoons lemon juice or
   to taste
1½ teaspoons raw cane sugar

Preheat the oven to 350°F.

Use your fingers to rub a little oil on both sides of all the eggplant pieces. Lay them on a large, nonstick baking sheet and bake for 10 minutes. Add the tofu to the baking sheet and cook for another 6 to 8 minutes, or until the eggplant pieces yield completely when pierced.

To make the dressing, whisk together the ingredients until the sugar has completely dissolved, then season to taste.

Place the hot, cooked eggplant, tofu, and quinoa into a large bowl along with the leaves, mint, and pine nuts (if using). Pour over the dressing, mix well, and serve.

# Warm Sweet Potato, Arugula, and Goat Cheese Salad

**VATA**
Fantastic for vata

**PITTA**
Good for pitta

**KAPHA**
Eat only occasionally

Sweet potatoes are really good for us as they contain lots of antioxidants, vitamins, and other healing properties. This salad is very grounding and nourishing, it is fantastic for vata but also good for pitta and only slightly increases kapha energy but in a positive way. It is a delicious salad—the sweetness of the potato, the peppery spices, the slight bitterness of the leaves, the lemony dressing, and the crunch of the almonds work really well together. The watercress is great for cleansing pitta and a good pungent green for warming up kapha and vata. Even though this recipe forms a side salad, I often eat a larger portion as a light meal in the summer months.

**Serves 2 as a small salad**

1 medium orange-fleshed sweet potato, diced into 1-inch cubes
1 small red onion, sliced into thin wedges
2 teaspoons vegetable oil
½ teaspoon panch phoran seeds (also called Bengali 5-seed mix)
Salt and freshly ground black pepper
1½ ounces small watercress leaves
⅛ cup whole almonds, blanched and lightly roasted and split through the middle
2 ounces soft goat cheese (omit this if you have a kapha imbalance)
Salt and freshly ground black pepper

**Dressing**
1¾ teaspoons lemon juice
4 teaspoons vegetable oil
½ teaspoon garlic paste

Preheat the oven to 375°F.

Place the potato and onion on a small baking sheet. Heat the oil in a small saucepan and add the seeds. When they have sizzled for 10 seconds over low heat, pour over the vegetables, season, and mix well. Place in the oven and roast for 45 to 50 minutes, or until soft.

Whisk together all the ingredients for the dressing and season with salt and lots of freshly ground black pepper.

When ready to serve, I pour the dressing straight on the baking sheet and toss well to coat, then throw in the leaves and almonds and continue to stir until all well amalgamated. Plate up and serve warm with the goat cheese crumbled on top.

# Middle Eastern Meze Plate

**Serves 4 to 5 meze size portions**

## Broiled Sesame Seed Chicken

2 teaspoons vegetable oil
1 fat garlic clove, made into a paste
4 teaspoons lemon juice
1½ teaspoons ground cumin
⅓ teaspoon salt
2 large chicken breasts, cut into cubes

**Sesame seed dressing**
4 teaspoons sesame seed paste (tahini)
4 teaspoons water
1 to 1½ tablespoons lemon juice
⅓ teaspoon garlic paste
Small handful of parsley, chopped
Salt and freshly ground black pepper

VATA Great for vata; good
    substitute for the hummus
PITTA Eat occasionally
KAPHA Good occasionally

This is a good option for vata instead of the hummus. Sesame seed paste is a little heating for pitta and heavy for kapha, so eat only occasionally.

Mix the oil, garlic, lemon, cumin, and salt together in a nonmetallic bowl. Add the chicken and marinate in a cool place for as long as possible. Stir the dressing ingredients together.

Soak four wooden skewers in water. Preheat the broiler to moderate temperature. Remove the chicken from the marinade and thread onto the skewers. Place the skewers directly on the broiler rack and cook for 7 to 8 minutes, or until done, turning halfway through.

## Herbed Bulgur Wheat

½ cup bulgur wheat, cooked according
    to package directions and drained
4 ounces flat-leaf parsley, tough stalks
    removed and the rest minced
1 ounce mint, leaves minced
1½ to 2½ tablespoons extra virgin
    olive oil (kapha should only
    use 1½ tablespoons)
2 to 3 teaspoons lemon juice
Salt and freshly ground black pepper
Good pinch of raw cane sugar
½ teaspoon ground cumin
½ scallion, finely sliced (kapha only)
Handful of pine nuts, lightly roasted
    (vata and pitta only)

VATA Suits vata with the pine nuts
PITTA Suits pitta with the pine nuts
KAPHA Suits kapha with scallion
    and less oil

Mint and parsley are both wonderful herbs to stimulate good digestion and mint also helps to calm the nerves. This salad is good for all doshas. Those with a kapha imbalance who are feeling a little sluggish can replace the bulgur wheat with quinoa.

Mix together all the ingredients, scallions (kapha only), and pine nuts (vata and pitta). Season and adjust the lemon juice to taste.

## Almond Green Beans

8½ ounces green beans
2 to 4 teaspoons vegetable or olive oil
    (2 teaspoons kapha, 3 teaspoons
    pitta, 4 teaspoons vata)
1 teaspoon cumin seeds
Scant ¼ cup almonds, blanched and split
    through middle (only 1 tablespoon
    for kapha)
Salt and freshly ground black pepper
1½ to 2 teaspoons lemon juice

VATA Suits vata with more oil
PITTA Suits pitta
KAPHA Suits kapha with fewer
    almonds

A very simple vegetable that is transformed with the almonds. Good for all doshas.

Cook the beans in boiling water for about 3 minutes, until tender but still crisp. Heat the oil in a nonstick skillet. Add the cumin seeds and cook until darkening. Add the almonds and stir-fry until lightly golden. Add the blanched beans, seasoning, and lemon juice to taste. Sauté to heat through.

## Healthy Hummus

1½ cups cooked chickpeas (set aside
    1 tablespoon for garnish)
2 to 3 tablespoons vegetable oil (vata
    add 3 tablespoons)
1½ tablespoons water
1 teaspoon ground cumin
2 small garlic cloves, peeled
1½ to 2 teaspoons sesame seed paste
    (tahini)
2½ to 3 tablespoons lemon juice
Salt and freshly ground black pepper

VATA Easier to digest than chickpeas
PITTA Suits all doshas
KAPHA Suits all doshas

This is a wonderful dish for kapha and pitta and even vata often find they can digest chickpeas as they have been pureed. Sesame seeds are nourishing for the body, bones, and immunity.

Blend all the ingredients together to make a fine paste. Season to taste, adjust the lemon juice if necessary, and serve topped with the reserved chickpeas.

**Opposite:** I love the variety of small bites that come as part of a Middle Eastern meze platter and there is no reason why this cannot be part of a healthy diet. I usually select two or three dishes and serve with griddled herbed flat breads (see page 141) or bought whole wheat pita.

# Poppy-Seed Crusted Tuna Niçoise Salad

**VATA**
Great for vata

**PITTA**
Omit vinegar, use more lemon juice

**KAPHA**
Eat occasionally with less dressing

**Serves 2**

2 small tuna steaks, about ½ inch thick
1½ teaspoons poppy seeds
1½ teaspoons vegetable oil
6 baby new potatoes
3½ ounces green beans
3-inch piece cucumber, peeled and finely sliced
8 black Niçoise olives
2 handfuls of salad greens
Salt and black pepper

**Lemon pistachio dressing**
1½ tablespoons lemon juice plus ¾ teaspoon for the marinade
3 tablespoons olive oil
1 teaspoon white wine vinegar
1 small garlic clove, chopped
1½ tablespoons water
Heaping 1 tablespoon pistachios, shelled weight

In my version of the famed salad I have omitted the eggs and anchovies as one complex protein at a time is enough for our digestion. Sea fish is quite heating so if you have a skin- or heat-related (pitta) problem, it is best avoided. This is a great dish for vata as most elements are cooked and it could be eaten warm. Cook the tuna all the way through as raw fish is not very Ayurvedic. This salad is fine for kapha on the odd occasion but use less dressing.

Boil the potatoes in their skins until tender. Add the beans, cook for 2 to 3 minutes, then drain. Pound or blend the dressing ingredients into a smooth paste. Separately toss the potatoes, beans, and cucumber in a little of the dressing.

Mix ¾ teaspoon each oil and lemon juice with some seasoning and rub over the tuna. Heat the remaining oil in a nonstick skillet. Sprinkle the poppy seeds over both sides of the tuna and pat them in. Place in the pan, cook over moderate heat for 2 minutes on each side. Slice the tuna and pour the pan juices into the remaining dressing. Make a bed of greens with neat piles of the other ingredients on top. Drizzle the remaining dressing over the tuna.

# Warm Cranberry Bean, Mozzarella, and Herb Salad

**PITTA**
Great for pitta

**KAPHA**
Great for a summer lunch

**Lemon, garlic, and parsley dressing**
3 to 4 tablespoons vegetable oil (kapha use 3 tablespoons)
⅓ cup finely sliced onion (¼ to ⅓ small onion)
2 medium to large garlic cloves, finely sliced
¾ teaspoon ground cumin
1½ to 2 tablespoons lemon juice (kapha use lesser amount)
¼ cup chopped flat-leaf parsley

1½ cups cooked cranberry beans (well-washed if canned, or see cooking instructions on page 57)
3 large handfuls of mixed lettuce greens
1 ounce endives, shredded lengthwise
1 large ball of good-quality mozzarella, pulled apart into chunky long shreds
1 large roasted red bell pepper, skinned and sliced
3¼-ounce cucumber, halved and finely sliced
Salt and freshly ground black pepper

**Serves 2**

A great salad for those with a pitta imbalance or a kapha imbalance as the cranberry beans and endives are great for both of them. This dish is not suitable for vata as it would be too hard to digest. It is okay for kapha at lunchtime (when digestion is at its peak) in the summer months and I have added some ground cumin to help digest the beans. You can buy the roasted red bell pepper from any deli counter or make your own by roasting the bell pepper in a very hot oven until the skin is blistered and blackened. Take out and cover with plastic wrap for 5 minutes. When cool enough to handle, peel off the skin. You can now use them but I like to brush them with olive oil and quickly cook them on a stovetop grill pan.

To make the dressing, heat the oil in a small pan. Add the onion and a little salt and cook over moderate heat until they are browning well and look dry and shriveled. Add the garlic, lower the heat, and cook for another 40 seconds. Add the lemon juice, parsley, beans, and black pepper, if using (kapha only). Stir together, taste, and adjust the seasoning and lemon. Toss together with the remaining salad ingredients and serve.

# Broiled Endive, Goat Cheese, and Beet Salad

VATA
See note on vata
imbalance

PITTA
Replace the beet with
dried figs

KAPHA
Great for kapha

This is a great salad to introduce some bitter flavors into kapha and pitta diets; bitter foods are very cleansing and detoxifying and should be eaten everyday. Beet is fantastic for the blood and great for vata and kapha, but can sometimes be a little heating for pitta so if you have a serious pitta imbalance, replace the beet with dried figs. This salad also works for vata, but for a serious vata imbalance, omit the endive and caramelize half a sliced red onion in 2 teaspoons of oil, then mix with the greens.

**Serves 2**

1 large endive or chicory, quartered
    lengthwise
4 fresh thyme sprigs
1 teaspoon vegetable oil
1 soft, flavorsome log of goat cheese
2 to 3 slices of bread of your choice
    (kapha ideally choose rye bread)
2 to 3 generous handfuls of red oakleaf
    or other soft salad greens
2 large cooked beet, peeled and
    cut into wedges (kapha and vata),
3 large dried figs, cut into wedges (pitta)

**Pitta dressing**
3 teaspoons olive oil
½ teaspoon lemon juice
Salt to taste
Good pinch of sugar

**Kapha dressing**
2 teaspoons olive oil
1 teaspoon balsamic vinegar
Salt to taste

**Vata dressing**
4 teaspoons olive oil
1½ teaspoons balsamic vinegar
Salt to taste

Preheat the broiler to 425°F, or to its highest setting.

Whisk together the dressing for your body type.

Place the endives in a small baking dish, top each with a sprig of thyme, and drizzle over the olive oil. Broil for 10 minutes, or until lightly browned in spots, turning over halfway.

Cut the goat cheese log into 6 to 8 slices ½ inch thick. From the bread, cut out the same number of circles the size of the log using a pastry cutter. Lightly broil the toast for 1 minute on each side.

Place the goat cheese slices on top of the toasted bread. Place on the broiler rack and broil for 4 minutes, or until the cheese is hot and browning in places.

Make a bed of salad greens on each plate. Top with the endives, beet, or dried figs, and top with the broiled goat cheese croutons. Drizzle with the dressing and serve hot.

# Broiled Tofu, Green Bean, Noodle, and Sesame Salad

**PITTA**
Use buckwheat
noodles

**KAPHA**
Use rice noodles

This is a delicious, substantial Japanese-inspired salad that is very good for kapha and pitta. It is low in fat but very nourishing with protein from tofu and lots of crunchy vegetables. This dish includes sesame seeds—an amazing seed credited with everything from keeping our bones health and building ojas to keeping us looking young. They are mildly heating so if you have a serious pitta imbalance, you can leave them out or eat only in the winter months. This salad isn't suitable for vata as it has lots of uncooked elements and tofu, which some vata types find hard to digest.

**Serves 2**

3¼ ounces green beans
7 ounces firm tofu, sliced horizontally
    to form two steaks
Salt and freshly ground black pepper
½ teaspoon sesame oil, plus extra for
    brushing tofu
1½ teaspoons sesame seeds
3¼ ounces snow peas
3¼ ounces sugar snap peas
1 small carrot, cut into thin strips
Handful of shredded red cabbage
2 ounces noodles (buckwheat noodles
    for kapha, rice noodles for pitta),
    cooked according to package
    directions (optional)
½ scallion, green parts sliced
    (kapha only)

**Dressing**
3½ ounces silken tofu
1½ teaspoons tamari
1½ teaspoons mirin
½ teaspoon superfine sugar
½ teaspoon ginger paste

Blanch the beans in a pan of boiling water for 2 to 3 minutes, or until crisp yet tender. Drain.

Heat a griddle, stovetop grill pan, or the broiler. Season the tofu steaks on both sides, brush with sesame oil, place on the hot griddle, grill pan, or under the broiler, and cook for 3 minutes on each side.

Meanwhile, lightly toast the sesame seeds in a dry skillet, keeping an eye on them as when they turn brown, they turn fast. Tip most of them (set aside a few for garnish) into a mortar and pestle and roughly crush.

Place the vegetables and noodles in a large bowl. Whisk or blend together the ingredients for the dressing, pour into the bowl, add the crushed sesame seeds, and toss well. Place the tofu on top, brush with sesame oil, and sprinkle over the sliced scallions and reserved sesame seeds. Serve.

# Chicken, Fennel, and Fava Bean Salad

 VATA
Serve warm for vata imbalance

 PITTA
Great for pitta

 KAPHA
Omit the avocado and eat in moderation

This is a delicious salad, full of wonderful flavors and textures. It's a great salad for pitta, but also good for vata in the summer and ideally at lunchtime when your digestion is at its best. Those with a vata imbalance can also serve this salad warm by sautéing the fennel and warming the fava beans. This salad is a little heavy for those with a kapha imbalance but would be suitable for a summer lunch without the avocado.

**Serves 2**

2 small chicken breasts, skinned
2 teaspoons vegetable oil
1 Boston lettuce or other soft lettuce
½ small avocado, peeled, pitted, and cut into small pieces (kapha should omit this)
¼ cup shelled fava beans, cooked
1 small fennel bulb, trimmed and finely sliced or shaved
Salt and freshly ground black pepper

**Creamy tarragon dressing**
2 tablespoons lemon juice
1½ tablespoons vegetable oil
2 tablespoons water
½ teaspoon raw cane sugar
½ garlic clove, grated
2 tablespoons pine nuts (those with a kapha imbalance may want to use half)
2 tarragon sprigs, leaves only

Preheat the oven to 350°F.

Season the chicken on both sides and cut three or four diagonal slashes through the thick parts of the breast. Heat the oil in an ovenproof pan and sear the breasts for 1 to 2 minutes on each side, or until well colored, then transfer to the oven to cook for 10 to 12 minutes, or until the chicken is cooked through. Check that the chicken is cooked through by piercing the thicker parts of the meat with the tip of a knife—the juices should run clear rather than pink.

To make the dressing, blend together all the ingredients except the tarragon until smooth, then season, and stir in the tarragon.

Mix together the ingredients for the salad. Slice the cooked chicken thinly on the diagonal. Place the chicken on the salad, drizzle over the dressing, toss, and serve.

# FISH

Fish and seafood are sweet, heavy, and warming. Traditionally, Ayurvedic doctors believe we should eat the small species of fish as larger ones have a higher degree of kapha, so eating them will bring more kapha into our bodies. Freshwater fish are the best option, followed by seawater (preferably deep-water fish as the surface water is often more polluted). Shellfish are comparatively more heating, but if you enjoy shellfish, try to partner them with foods with cooling properties.

People with a vata imbalance can benefit from the nourishment and heat that fish provide, but even for these body types, it is not a good idea to eat fish everyday, as a varied diet is the healthiest. The heat of the fish does counter the coolness of kapha, but kapha body types should stick to light food and fish is considered comparatively heavy. Kapha should avoid oily fish and eat light white fish. The heat of seafood is particularly bad for the already-hot pitta body types so eat sparingly (chicken is a better option). Choose recipes that include cooling ingredients to balance this heat, such as cilantro, coconut, and mint.

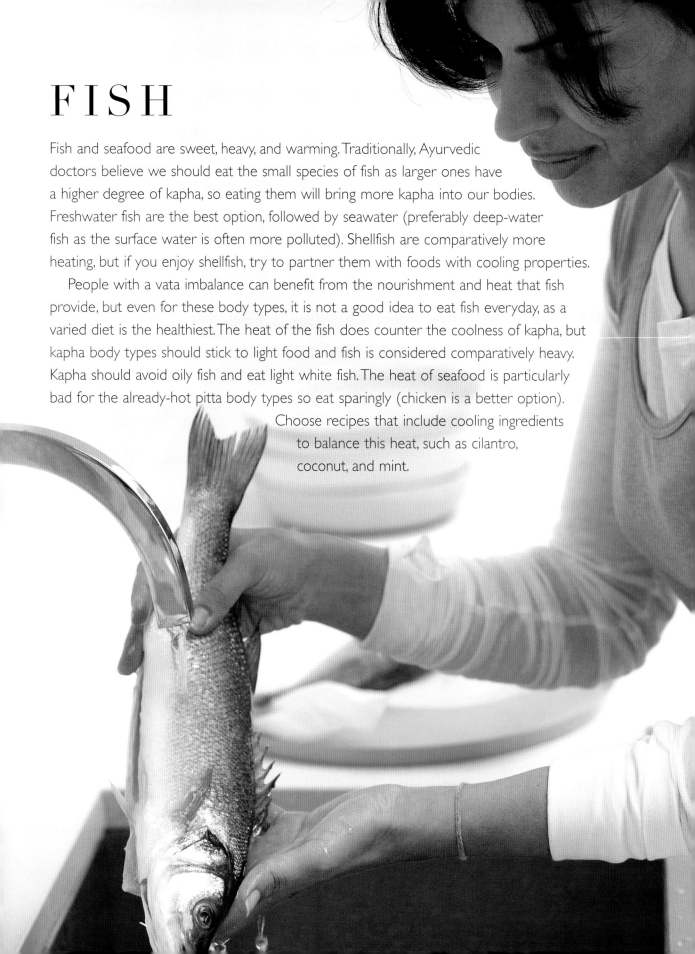

# Fish and Saffron Stew with Parsley Mayonnaise

**VATA**
Can add garlic, lemon, and paprika to the mayo

**PITTA**
Good for pitta

**KAPHA**
For kapha imbalance, see note below

Saffron is a great spice to use with fish as it helps to cool its heating properties. This dish is based upon a French-style fish stew but without the wine (a very strong and penetrating taste which pitta should avoid, even in food) and cream (dairy and animal proteins do not mix well). It is still delicious and nourishing and light enough for all the three body types, although those with a kapha imbalance should take the Ayurvedic option (see below, it is still delicious). I would serve this only with a little crusty bread on the side (buttered for vata and pitta only). Vata can add a little garlic paste, lemon, and paprika to the mayonnaise.

**Serves 2**

1½ tablespoons ghee or butter (kapha should use ¾ tablespoon vegetable oil)
½ medium onion, sliced
¼ to ½ head of fennel
1 small carrot, chopped
⅓ leek, (white parts only), sliced and washed
1 large thyme sprig
1 garlic clove, sliced
⅓ teaspoon ground coriander
⅓ teaspoon fennel seeds, ground
Salt
1½ cups fish stock
⅔ cup water
A fat pinch of saffron threads
2 fillets of firm white fish, such as sea bass, haddock, cod, red mullet, or monkfish
Handful of flat-leaf parsley, chopped
1 rounded tablespoon mayonnaise

Heat the ghee, butter, or oil in a medium nonstick saucepan. Add the onion, fennel, carrots, leek, and thyme. Sauté gently for 8 to 10 minutes, or until the onion is soft and starting to color. Spoon out a quarter of the vegetables and set aside. Add the garlic and spices to the pan, season with salt, and sauté for 30 seconds. Then add the fish stock and water and crumble in the saffron.

Bring to a boil, then simmer gently for 12 to 15 minutes, uncovered— you want to end up with 1½ to 1¾ cups of well-flavored liquid. Add in the fish and reserved vegetables, bring to a simmer, cover, and cook gently for 3 to 4 minutes, or until the fish is cooked. Spoon out the fish and place in the serving bowl.

Stir the parsley into the mayonnaise, then stir into the fish stew, adjust the seasoning, and ladle into the serving bowl over the fish.

**Strict Ayurveda**

To follow strict Ayurveda principles, before adding the fish to the stew, blend the vegetables to a fine puree, then adjust the seasoning and consistency of the soup by adding or cooking off excess liquid. Add the fish and reserved vegetables back into the soup and cook, covered as above. Stir in the parsley and serve.

# Creamy Salmon, Potato, and Bean Packages

VATA
Good for vata

PITTA
Good for pitta

KAPHA
Use fewer potatoes
and add more beans

A classic combination of salmon, potatoes, and dill, with the addition of a few nigella seeds which go really well with fish. I have used a little store-bought mayo to add the touch of creaminess that we can miss when eating an Ayurvedic diet (Ayurveda says dairy and animal protein should not be mixed). This dish is great for vata and pitta constitutions and kapha can lighten by reducing the amount of potatoes and doubling the amount of beans, which also means they can use a little less dressing as the potatoes absorb a lot of it. New potatoes are easier to digest than many other potato varieties.

**Serves 2**

11 ounces baby new potatoes
2 ounces green beans
1½ teaspoons ghee or vegetable oil
¼ teaspoon nigella seeds
2 shallots, sliced
1 fat garlic clove, peeled and left
    whole, but lightly crushed to release
    its flavor
2 salmon fillets
Small handful of baby watercress

**Dressing**
2 tablespoons olive oil
1½ tablespoons mayonnaise
1 teaspoon lemon juice
¼ ounce dill, leaves chopped
Salt and freshly ground black pepper
    (pitta please omit)

Preheat the oven to 350°F.

Halve the potatoes and boil until soft. Remove from the pan and blanch the beans for 1 to 2 minutes.

Heat the oil in a small nonstick saucepan and add the nigella seeds. When they have sizzled for 15 seconds, add the shallots and garlic and cook over low heat for 6 to 7 minutes, or until soft and browning at the edges. Remove the garlic.

Meanwhile, whisk together the ingredients for the dressing, adding 2 teaspoons of water, and season.

Toss the beans, potatoes, and onions with the dressing. Cut two pieces of parchment paper or foil, about 12 inches square. Place half the vegetables in the middle of each paper. Season the fish and place on top, skin side up. Enclose the package by making a loose envelope, tightly folding in the edges all the way around so that the filling is entirely enclosed. Place on a baking sheet and bake for 14 to 16 minutes. Check the fish is done; if not, place back in the oven for a few more minutes.

Remove the skin from the fish, garnish with the watercress, and serve with the vegetables.

# Fragrant Coconut Fish Curry

**VATA**
Great for vata

**PITTA**
Good for pitta
occasionally

This mildly spiced curry is wonderful for vata as it is creamy and soft and warming from the spices. Coconut milk is a wonderful ingredient to pair with fish as it is cooling (fish is quite heating), so this is a good way for those with a pitta imbalance to enjoy fish. If you are pitta, grind the seeds where mentioned below for a milder dish. Use any white fish fillets in this dish. You can also add some fresh peas or other vegetables to the curry. Serve with rice.

**Serves 2**

1 tablespoon vegetable oil or ghee
1-inch cinnamon shard
3 cloves
⅓ teaspoon mustard seeds
8 fenugreek seeds, optional (omit if you have a strong pitta imbalance)
5 black peppercorns (omit if you have a strong pitta imbalance)
7 curry leaves
½ small to medium onion, thinly sliced
1½ teaspoons garlic paste
1½ teaspoons ginger paste
¼ teaspoon ground turmeric
Salt
⅔ cup coconut milk
9 ounces firm white fish fillets of your choice, cut into large cubes
1 teaspoon lemon juice or to taste

Heat the oil in a small nonstick saucepan. Add the whole spices and cook until the mustard seeds pop. Add the curry leaves, immediately follow with the onion, and cook until soft.

Add the garlic and ginger and stir-fry for 1 minute, adding a splash of water if it looks like it might burn. Stir in the turmeric and season to taste with salt. Add generous ⅓ cup water and simmer for 7 minutes, or until quite reduced. Add the coconut milk, bring to a boil, and cook for 2 to 3 minutes. Taste and adjust seasoning and check the amount of sauce in the pan—it should be creamy but not thick (cook off any excess water or add a little more from the kettle).

Stir in the lemon juice, then add your fish in one layer and cook on gentle simmer for 4 to 5 minutes, or until done, shaking the pan from time to time. Serve with rice.

# Star Anise and Ginger Steamed Fish

**VATA**
Omit the chile and
add butter or ghee

**PITTA**
Omit the chile and
add butter or ghee

**KAPHA**
Great for kapha
imbalance

This is a really quick, really light midweek meal. If you do not have a steamer or you are making larger quantities, you can cook the fish in the oven in an enclosed package (foil or parchment), adding another teaspoon of water. This is excellent for those with a kapha imbalance as it is a light but pungent dish. It also works for pitta and vata—leave out the chile but you can add a teaspoon of ghee/butter to the dish as it cooks (vata can add ¼ teaspoon sesame oil too). Serve with steamed rice.

**Serves 1 (can easily be doubled)**

1 fillet of fish such as flounder, sole, sea bass, bream, or other flat fish
3½ ounces sprouting broccoli or other greens, steamed along with or before the fish

**Marinade**
1½ teaspoons light soy sauce
¾ teaspoon dark soy sauce
7 drops sesame oil
1¼ teaspoons Chinese cooking wine
Good pinch of sugar
2-inch length of scallion, cut into fine julienne (kapha—set aside a little of the green to garnish)
½ teaspoon ginger, cut into thin slices or fine julienne
1 garlic clove, crushed well to release its juices
⅛ to ¼ red Chinese chile, seeded and sliced (adds lots of flavor)
1 star anise

Mix together the ingredients for the marinade in a nonmetallic bowl and add 1 teaspoon of water. Press on the aromatics a little to help them release their flavor. Pour over the fish and let marinate in a cool place for 20 to 30 minutes if possible.

Heat 1 inch of water in a wide steamer or a wok with a wire rack set inside. Place the fish with its marinade in a small plate that fits in the steamer (or make an aluminum foil boat for it). Place in the steamer, cover, and cook for 4 to 6 minutes, or until the fish is cooked through. Remove the garlic and pour the rest of the marinade over the fish. If you are kapha, garnish with the reserved scallion.

# Lightly Spiced Smoked Trout Tortillas

VATA
Good for vata

PITTA
Eat only occasionally

KAPHA
Good for kapha; ideally
use corn tortillas

These simple tortillas burst with the complex flavors of the fresh vegetables, smoky fish, and a little spice. This dish is good for vata and kapha but with slightly different vegetables (see below). For those with a serious pitta imbalance, it should be made ideally without the tomatoes, mustard seeds, black pepper, and red onion, but do add a little extra mayonnaise and sharpen with lemon juice.

**Serves 2 (can easily be doubled)**

2 smoked trout fillets
2 flour or corn tortillas (preferably
   corn for kapha and flour for vata)
1 to 3 teaspoons vegetable oil (kapha
   1 teaspoon; pitta 2 teaspoons;
   vata 3 teaspoons)
1/4 teaspoon mustard seeds
1/8 teaspoon nigella seeds
31/4 ounces red cabbage, finely shredded
   (vata should omit; add some
   shredded cucumber instead)
Large handful of baby watercress

**Dressing**
1 rounded tablespoon mayonnaise
2 teaspoons lime or lemon juice
1 small tomato, chopped
1 thin slice of red onion, halved to
   make two sets of moon-shaped rings
1 large handful of cilantro, roughly
   chopped
1/4 to 1/3 avocado (vata only), peeled,
   pitted, and chopped
1/3 teaspoon ground cumin
1/8 teaspoon minced garlic, optional
Salt and freshly ground black pepper

Preheat the oven to 350°F.

To make the dressing, stir together the mayonnaise, lime juice, tomato, red onion, cilantro, avocado (if using), ground cumin, and garlic. Season to taste.

Place the trout fillets on a baking sheet and place in the oven for 5 minutes to warm through. Wrap the tortillas in foil and add for the final 2 minutes.

Heat the oil in a nonstick skillet, tilting it to one side. Add the seeds and once they sizzle, add the cabbage (if using) and stir-fry for 2 to 3 minutes, just until it loses its rawness. If you are vata and not using cabbage, add the seeds, oil, and shredded cucumber to the mayonnaise.

Place the watercress in a line along the middle of the tortilla. Top with the cabbage, then add the fish and cover with the dressing. Roll and eat immediately (it also tastes good as a cold wrap).

# Provençal Trout with Lemon Salsa Verde

VATA
Great for vata

PITTA
Omit the capers

**Serves 2**

**Lemon salsa verde**
3 tablespoons olive oil
3 teaspoons lemon juice
1 rounded tablespoon chopped parsley
¾ tablespoon each shredded mint and basil leaves
2 teaspoons capers, well washed (vata only)
1 small garlic clove, made into a paste

2 heaping tablespoons black olives, (packed in oil not brine), drained and minced
⅓ teaspoon lemon zest
1 small garlic clove, made into a paste
1 tablespoon olive oil
2 to 3 slices white bread, crumbed (scant 1¼ cups)
1 medium trout, butterflied (bones removed but fish kept intact—your fish supplier can do this for you)
Salt and freshly ground black pepper
2 rosemary sprigs, lightly crushed

Freshwater fish is a good ayurvedic food choice as it is less heating than seawater fish. This is a really simple dish to cook and great for vata with simple ingredients and flavors which they should find easy to digest, nourishing, and grounding. This dish is also good for pitta, although only to be eaten occasionally and pitta should omit the capers (which are quite sour) from the dressing. This dish is a little too rich for those with a kapha imbalance. Serve with steamed vegetables.

Preheat the oven to 350°F.

Mix together the olives, lemon zest, garlic paste, and half the olive oil. Stir in the bread crumbs. Season the fish inside and out, place the filling inside, and fold the fish over so it is back in its original shape. Place on a baking sheet, top with the rosemary, and drizzle over the remaining oil. Bake on the middle shelf of the oven for 25 to 30 minutes, or until the fish is cooked.

Stir together the ingredients for the salsa verde. Season to taste and serve drizzled over the fish.

# Broiled Sardines with "Sauce Vierge"

VATA
Great for vata

PITTA
Eat only occasionally; balance with cooling foods for the rest of the day

**Serves 2**

2 large or 4 small sardines, cleaned and boned, or 2 large mackerel fillets
2 slices from a country-style loaf, toasted

**"Sauce vierge"**
5 baby tomatoes
2½ tablespoons olive oil
2 tablespoons minced shallot or red onion
1 fat garlic clove, chopped
1½ teaspoons lemon juice
Salt and lots of freshly ground black pepper
1 teaspoon chopped parsley
1 teaspoon chopped tarragon

Broiled sardines are a wonderful, oily fish that is fantastic for a vata imbalance. Ayurveda says that if you eat fish, opt for smaller species, such as these sardines (you can also make this dish with mackerel fillets or any firm white fish). The dressing is usually served raw or "virgin," but I have cooked it to make it less sharp and easier to digest. Serve on toast or with cooked vegetables, such as green beans, or a simple well-dressed salad in the summer.

Preheat the broiler to moderate heat. Boil the tomatoes in a pan of water for 2 minutes. Spoon out and remove the skins.

Heat the oil in a small nonstick pan, add the onion, and cook over high heat until golden around the edges. Add the garlic, reduce the heat, and cook gently for 30 to 50 seconds, or until the garlic smells cooked. Take off the heat. Quarter the tomatoes and add to the pan with the lemon juice, seasoning, and herbs. Adjust the seasoning and tartness to taste.

Place the fish on a baking sheet, skin side up, and broil for 3 to 4 minutes (5 minutes for mackerel), turn over, and broil for 1 minute, or until done. Place the fish on the toast and spoon over the sauce.

# Steam-Baked Fish with Mint, Cilantro, and Coconut

 **VATA**
Good for vata with black pepper

 **PITTA**
Great for pitta

 **KAPHA**
Eat only occasionally; avoid if you have a strong kapha imbalance

**Serves 2**

2 firm white fillets
½ teaspoon ghee, optional

**Herb paste**
1½ ounces creamed coconut
5 tablespoons mint leaves
¾ ounce cilantro leaves and stalks
1½ to 1¾ teaspoons lime or lemon juice
1 small garlic clove
½ teaspoon ground coriander
⅓ teaspoon ground cumin
Good pinch of sugar
Salt to taste

This is a really easy way to cook fish and both the cilantro and mint are fantastic herbs to help us digest this protein. The coconut is wonderfully cooling so this is a great dish for pitta in particular but also good for vata, who can add a little freshly ground black pepper to give the dish a little kick. The cooling coconut makes it a little cold and heavy for those with a kapha imbalance, but when you feel more in balance it is definitely worth a try. Serve with steamed rice and a suitable vegetable.

Blend together all the ingredients for the paste, adding 5 to 6 tablespoons water until you have a fine puree. Taste and adjust the seasoning (overseason slightly as the fish will draw out the salt).

Cut out two large squares of strong aluminum foil. Place the fish in the middle of the double layer of foil, skin side down, and spread the paste over the top and the ghee on top of the paste (if using). Wrap up the fish package so no steam can escape (I fold in the edges a couple of times all the way around). Let marinate for 15 minutes while you heat the oven to 350°F.

Bake for 12 to 14 minutes, or until the fish is cooked. Remove the skin from the fish and serve.

# Broiled Sole with Lemon, Almonds, and Parsley

 **VATA**
Suits all doshas

 **PITTA**
Suits all doshas

 **KAPHA**
Omit the ghee or butter

**Serves 2**

2 English sole fillets
4 teaspoons lemon juice
½ teaspoon grated lemon zest
1 teaspoon ghee or butter (kapha leave out)
2 teaspoons vegetable oil
2 garlic cloves, made into a paste
Salt
1½ tablespoons slivered almonds
1 heaping tablespoon chopped parsley

This simple dish is perfect for midweek suppers. It is really easy to prepare and quick to cook. It can work for all the body types, but serve with grains or vegetables to suit your own dosha. The fish is also delicious sprinkled with fresh bread crumbs instead of the almonds. Serve with fresh vegetables.

Preheat the broiler to 350°F, or medium heat.

Rinse the fish fillets and pat dry, check for any bones, and remove if necessary. Place the fillets in a small, snug baking dish.

In a bowl, whisk together the lemon juice and zest, ghee (if using), oil, 2 tablespoons water, garlic, and salt and spread over the fish, turning once to coat. Sprinkle the almonds on the top and place under the broiler (on one of the lower racks if possible) and broil for 5 to 6 minutes, or until the fish is cooked through and the almonds have slightly browned. Transfer to your plate, stir the parsley into the juices in the pan, and pour over the fish and serve.

**Opposite:** Broiled Sole with Lemon, Almonds, and Parsley

# CHICKEN

Chicken is sweet, heating, and heavy on the body. It is comparatively easier to digest and, therefore, assimilate than red meat, as well as being lighter in quality. It is also less heating than seafood. So, as far as animal proteins go, chicken is one of the better options, especially for pitta, along with turkey which you can substitute for chicken in these recipes. I would advise removing the skin for both kapha and pitta; for vata, it is optional. If you do opt to keep the skin on, remember to brown any chicken that is going to be braised or you will end up with soft, unappetizing skin.

# Chicken, Broccoli, and Pea Curry

**VATA**
Great for vata

**PITTA**
Good for pitta

**KAPHA**
A rare occasional treat; opt
for the vegetarian version

**Serves 3 to 4**

1 ounce Thai basil or normal basil
1½ cups coconut milk
5 kaffir lime leaves
1½ to 2 teaspoons sugar or to taste
2 to 3 teaspoons Thai fish sauce
1¼ cups water
5 ounces purple sprouting or tender
    stem broccoli
2 large chicken breasts, skinned and
    cut into thick slivers, going with
    the grain
2 ounces snow peas
½ cup peas, fresh or frozen
Salt to taste

**Paste**
1 tablespoon vegetable oil
2 shallots, sliced
1 lemongrass stalk, bitter outer
    layers removed and inner tender
    white parts sliced
3 large garlic cloves, peeled
½-inch piece of galangal or ginger,
    roughly chopped
⅓ ounce cilantro stalks
1 to 2 green chiles (pitta please omit)

The lemongrass paste that forms the base of this curry balances doshas, warms the coolness of the coconut milk, and helps to digest the chicken. Cilantro is a wonderful herb for digestion and also for removing heavy metals and toxins from the body. This is a wonderful dish for vata and also good for pitta as the coconut milk is cooling, although I do think it is still quite heavy so more of a treat than an everyday meal. You can change the vegetables according to your list and what's in season. You can also make this vegetarian by using firm tofu instead of the chicken and using soy sauce instead of the fish sauce. Kapha, I'm so sorry to say that this dish is a little heavy and sweet for your body type so should only be eaten as the odd occasional treat. Serve with basmati rice.

To make the paste, heat the oil in a small saucepan and sauté the shallots until soft. Blend along with the remaining paste ingredients, 1 teaspoon of the basil, and 2 tablespoons of water until smooth. If necessary, scrape into a mortar and pestle and pound to finish it off.

Place the paste back in the saucepan and stir-fry for 3 to 4 minutes over moderate heat. Add coconut milk and bring to a boil. Add the lime leaves, sugar, fish sauce, and water and bring to a boil, then simmer for 3 to 4 minutes.

Add the broccoli and chicken and cook on low heat for 4 minutes. Add the remaining basil, plus the snow peas and peas. Bring back to a boil, adjust the seasoning, and add a splash of water if necessary for a loose, creamy consistency.

# Moroccan Braised Chicken with Dates and Vegetables

**VATA**
Great for vata

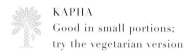

**PITTA**
Great for pitta

**KAPHA**
Good in small portions;
try the vegetarian version

This is a delicious Moroccan-inspired dish but without the traditional chickpeas (in Ayurveda we should try to limit the types of protein in a dish to just one) and without the strong preserved lemons. This dish is great for vata as it is unctuous and soft but can also work for healthy pitta body types with fewer spices. The vegetables lighten the dish and the flavorful broth is absolutely perfect with simple herb couscous, barley couscous, quinoa, or rice. Kapha can also enjoy this curry but should serve it without heavy grains or opt for the vegetarian version.

**Serves 4**

1½ to 2½ tablespoons vegetable oil
(kapha 1½ tablespoons, pitta
2 tablespoons, vata 2½ tablespoons)
1 medium to large onion, sliced
4 fat garlic cloves, grated into a paste
¾ teaspoon ginger paste
¾ teaspoon caraway seeds
½ teaspoon sweet paprika (for color)
4 small chicken thighs, bone in, skinned
and trimmed of all fat
2 cups chicken stock or vegetable stock
Salt and lots of freshly ground black
pepper
2 teaspoons tomato paste
1 small carrot, sliced on the diagonal
1 small zucchini, sliced on the diagonal
6 large dates, quartered lengthwise,
or other dried fruit (e.g. figs or
apricots)
Large handful of parsley, chopped

**Spice blend**
2-inch cinnamon shard
1½ teaspoons sesame seeds
1¼ teaspoons cumin seeds

To make the spice blend, grind the cinnamon, sesame, and cumin seeds together to make a fine powder—this is quite a quick job if you use a mortar and pestle.

Heat the oil in a large saucepan, add the onion, and cook gently until soft and coloring at the edges. Add the garlic and ginger and cook for 1 to 2 minutes, or until it smells cooked. Add a splash of water if it looks as though it may burn. Stir in the spice blend, the caraway seeds, and the paprika.

Add the chicken, stock, seasoning, and tomato paste. Bring to a boil and simmer gently, covered, for 18 minutes. Add the carrot, cover, and cook for about 8 minutes. Add the zucchini (or other vegetables) and cook for 6 to 7 minutes, or until the chicken and vegetables are all done. Stir in the dates and adjust the liquid quantity by cooking off excess water or adding a splash from the kettle. Stir in the parsley and serve.

**Vegetarian version**
Omit the chicken, use vegetable stock, add a few other vegetables, and stir in ½ to ¾ can of chickpeas or generous ¼ cup dried chickpeas, soaked overnight and cooked (they normally take 1½ hours).

# Persian Chicken with Saffron Rice Pilaf

**VATA**
Easy to digest for vata

**PITTA**
Good for pitta imbalance

**KAPHA**
Eat only small portions

This is a great dish, inspired by the simple, clean flavors of Persia. It is really good for pitta imbalances as saffron reduces pitta in the body and dates are great for cleansing the blood (a prolonged imbalanced pitta can lead to blood disorders). This dish is also good for vata as the saffron is nourishing and the rice easy to digest (you can add a little more ghee or butter). It contains a little too much of the "sweet" taste (chicken and rice are both "sweet") for kapha, but you can serve small portions with lots of vegetables on the side and use chicken breast instead of thighs.

**Serves 2**

12-ounce poussin (baby chicken), skinned and jointed (ask your butcher), or 2 large chicken thighs, skinned and 3 slashes cut on the surface

**Marinade**
2 tablespoons vegetable oil
2 tablespoons chicken stock, optional but improves flavor, or use water
¼ medium onion, chopped (use remainder in the rice)
1 tablespoon lemon juice
¾ teaspoon ground cumin
½ teaspoon ground cinnamon
2 tablespoons mint leaves

**Saffron rice**
½ cup basmati rice
Good pinch of saffron
1 tablespoon ghee or vegetable oil
1 bay leaf
1 large cinnamon stick
4 green cardamom pods
½ medium onion, sliced
1 garlic clove, minced
Scant 1 cup water or chicken stock (more flavor)
Salt
2 dates, pitted and sliced or chopped into large pieces

Mix together all the ingredients for the marinade. Add the chicken, stir well to coat, and let marinate for as long as possible (it is really important for the chicken to have time to absorb flavors, so overnight in the refrigerator is best). Bring back to room temperature before roasting.

Preheat the oven to 350°F. Scrape the marinade off the chicken and strain all the solids so that just the flavored oil remains. Place this in a baking dish, top with the chicken, and bake for 20 minutes for poussin or 30 minutes for thighs, or until done. Baste regularly with the oil.

Meanwhile, wash the basmati rice and let soak. Infuse the saffron in 2 tablespoons of hot water for 15 minutes.

To make the rice, heat the ghee or oil in a medium saucepan. Add the spices and cook for 20 seconds, then follow with the onion and cook until golden brown and slightly caramelized. Add the garlic and cook for 40 seconds, follow with the drained rice, water or stock, and saffron water. Season to taste (taste the water, it should be only slightly salty).

Bring to a boil, stir in the dates, reduce the heat to the lowest setting, cover tightly, and cook, undisturbed, for 9 minutes. Check one grain; if it's not done, cook for another minute or two. Turn off the heat and let steam for 5 minutes. Fluff up with a fork and serve topped with the chicken and drizzled with pan juices.

# Chicken and Cooling Herb Curry

VATA
Suits all doshas

PITTA
Suits all doshas

KAPHA
Suits all doshas

**Serves 3 to 4**

2 tablespoons ghee or vegetable oil (kapha, use half)
I small onion, sliced
1-pound 10-ounce chicken, skinned and jointed
1 to 2 green chiles, pierced with knife (pitta omit)

**Herb paste**
2½ ounces cilantro leaves and whole stalks
3 teaspoons lemon juice
2½ teaspoons mint leaves
2 fat garlic cloves, peeled
¼-ounce piece ginger
1½ tablespoons pistachios
¾ teaspoon cumin seeds
¾ teaspoon fennel seeds, ground
1 teaspoon ground coriander
Salt

This wonderful curry is cooked with cilantro and mint, both of which have cooling properties to balance the heat in the chicken and aid digestion. I use small chicken or poussin with the bones in, as the flavor from the bones really rounds off the sauce. If you are using normal chicken, add chicken stock instead of water. The sauce ingredients are great for all doshas. Serve with spelt rotis, broiled flat breads, or basmati rice. Kapha can serve with quinoa, millet, or pearl barley to soak up the gravy.

Blend the paste to a fine puree, adding salt to taste and a good splash of water to bind it together.

Heat the oil in a medium nonstick pan. Add the onion and cook for 8 minutes, or until golden. Add the chicken and brown briefly. Add the chiles (if using) and paste, stir well, season, and add water to come three-quarters of the way up the chicken. Bring to a boil, then reduce the heat, cover, and simmer, stirring occasionally, for 20 to 25 minutes, or until the chicken is cooked. Check after 15 minutes to see if the pan needs more water. The resulting gravy should be quite creamy. Season and serve.

# Stir-Fried Chicken with Beans and Peanuts

VATA
Good for vata

PITTA
Eat only occasionally

KAPHA
Good for kapha

**Serves 4**

1½ to 2½ tablespoons vegetable oil (vata use 2½ tablespoons)
½ teaspoon brown mustard seeds
8 large curry leaves
I small red onion, sliced
1 green chile, pierced with the tip of a knife (kapha only)
1¼ teaspoons ginger paste
3 garlic cloves, made into a paste
Salt and ¼ teaspoon freshly ground black pepper
3 chicken breasts, skinned, cut into 1-inch cubes
5 ounces green beans, sliced into long strips diagonally
1 to 2 tablespoons roasted peanuts, roughly ground (kapha use 1 tablespoon)
¾ teaspoon garam masala
½ teaspoon dry mango powder or lemon juice

This is a full-flavored South Indian-inspired dish which balances kapha and decreases vata. The spices aid digestion of the chicken, but if the spices and peanuts make it too heating for a pitta imbalance use cumin seeds instead of mustard seeds and add pine nuts or pumpkin seeds instead of peanuts. Serve with spelt rotis (see page 137), rice or as it is for a light meal.

Heat the oil in a small nonstick pan. Add the mustard seeds. Once they pop, add the curry leaves, onion, and chile. Stir-fry over high heat for 1 to 2 minutes. Lower the heat, add the ginger, garlic, and salt, and stir-fry for 30 to 40 seconds, or until the garlic smells cooked.

Add the chicken pieces, brown well over moderate heat, and add a splash of water. Cook, covered, for 2 minutes. Add the beans and cook, stirring often, for 3 minutes, or until cooked through. Check that the chicken is cooked through, then add the peanuts, pepper, garam masala, and mango powder or lemon juice. If the pan is looking dry, add a splash of hot water from the kettle and serve.

# Cornmeal-Crusted Chicken

A simple dish which is perfect for those with a kapha constitution as cornmeal is a drying grain and this oven-fried chicken is light and drying on the system (kapha should aim to eat "dry" meals at night). I like to serve this dish with Sautéed Corn with Peppers (see page 132), but you can choose any vegetables from your list. You can also make this with turkey breast which is lower in fat but also larger, so use one breast and slice on the diagonal before flattening.

**Serves 2**

2 small chicken breasts, skinned
1 tablespoon vegetable oil
Salt and lots of freshly ground black pepper
Lime wedges

**Marinade**
1¼ teaspoons lemon juice
⅓ teaspoon ground cumin
¾ teaspoons garlic paste
1½ tablespoons minced onion
2 teaspoons vegetable oil

**Coating**
3 tablespoons fresh bread crumbs
1½ tablespoons fine cornmeal
1 teaspoon thyme
¼ teaspoon garlic salt
⅓ teaspoon ground cumin
¼ teaspoon garam masala, optional, but very good with it
1½ teaspoons chopped parsley

Place the chicken breasts between two sheets of parchment paper. Using a rolling pin or other heavy instrument, flatten the chicken evenly until it is ⅝ inch thick. Mix together the ingredients for the marinade and season to taste. Coat the chicken well in the mix and let marinate, covered, in a nonmetallic dish in the refrigerator for as long as possible (I leave it overnight or for the day).

Preheat the oven to 350°F. Pour half the oil into a small roasting pan and place in the oven to heat up.

Stir together the ingredients for the coating. Season to taste with salt and black pepper.

Remove all the excess marinade from the chicken, making sure you remove all the onion. Press both sides of the chicken into the coating so you have an even layer of coating all over. Place in the hot roasting pan, drizzle over the remaining oil, and bake for 10 to 12 minutes, or until the chicken is cooked through. Serve with a wedge of lime.

# Greek-Style Chicken with Lemon, Potatoes, and Garlic

VATA
Very good for vata

PITTA
Good for pitta

KAPHA
Use skinless breast
instead of thigh

**Serves 4**

1 pound 2 ounces new potatoes, boiled and halved lengthwise
1 large red onion, cut into wedges
12 small asparagus spears
6 fat garlic cloves, minced
½ small lemon, cut into 3 wedges
2 tablespoons vegetable oil
Salt and lots of freshly ground black pepper
1 teaspoon ground cinnamon
4 large chicken thighs, bone in and skinned
1 tablespoon oregano (or a few thyme sprigs)
12 small black olives
⅔ cup chicken stock
2 handfuls of parsley, chopped (if using thyme rather than oregano)

This is an easy dish inspired by the Greek way of roasting chicken with lemon and garlic. It is light and filling and delicious as a summer or spring meal with salad for pitta or vegetables for vata. Don't be scared off by the amount of garlic in the food—it will be very mellow by the time it is cooked. This dish is a little heavy for those with a kapha imbalance but they can make it with fewer potatoes, breast of chicken, a little less oil, and more vegetables to lighten the meal.

Preheat the oven to 350°F.

Toss together the vegetables, garlic, 2 wedges of the lemon, oil, a little seasoning (the stock and olives have more), cinnamon, and chicken. Place in a baking dish and tuck in the oregano. Bake for 30 minutes, basting the chicken occasionally with any pan juices and tossing the vegetables around a little.

Add the olives and stock, place back in the oven, and cook for another 10 minutes, or until the chicken is cooked through. Stir in the parsley (if using) and serve.

# Braised Chicken with Dill and Lemon

VATA
Suits all doshas

PITTA
Suits all doshas

KAPHA
Suits all doshas

**Serves 2**

Olive or vegetable oil (2 teaspoons for kapha, 1 tablespoon for pitta, vata can add a little more or some butter at the end)
2 chicken breasts, skinned
1 small onion, finely sliced
1 fat garlic clove, minced
Salt and ½ teaspoon freshly ground black pepper (pitta please halve)
Generous ⅓ cup chicken stock
1½ ounces dill, minced
1 tablespoon lemon juice
A little butter for vata

This summery dish has simple but well-defined flavors. I like to cook the chicken whole and then slice it before serving for a neater dish. You do need good-quality stock in this dish to round off the flavors. Dill is a fantastic herb for all three doshas; it reduces pitta and kapha and is neutral on vata. Serve with some steamed greens and peeled new potatoes, simple basmati rice, or a hunk of bread on the side. This dish can work for all three doshas.

Heat the oil in a medium nonstick pan. Add the chicken breasts and brown on both sides, remove from the pan, and set aside. Add the onions and cook gently until very soft. Add the garlic and sauté for 40 to 50 seconds over low heat. Season well and add the chicken back to the pan with the stock. Bring to a boil, then reduce the heat, cover, and cook for 8 to 10 minutes, or until the chicken is cooked through.

Add the dill and lemon juice, cover, and cook for 2 minutes; vata can stir in butter for added richness. The dish should have some pan juices (loosen with warm water from the kettle if necessary or take out the chicken and boil off any extra liquid). Serve.

**Opposite:** Greek-Style Chicken with Lemon, Potatoes, and Garlic

# Chicken Laksa with Rice Noodles

VATA
Great for vata imbalance

PITTA
Suitable for pitta

This dish is somewhat like a Malaysian laksa, but much lighter and easier to digest. This is a wonderful dish for those with a vata imbalance as it is creamy, unctuous, and grounding. It is also suitable for pitta as the coconut milk and fresh herbs all balance pitta. Rice noodles are easier to digest than wheat noodles and are very grounding. This is not a great dish for kapha as it can be a little heavy for them, although you could lighten the dish by substituting firm tofu instead of the chicken (also good for pitta) and using buckwheat noodles and less coconut milk.

**Serves 4**

1 tablespoon vegetable or coconut oil
1 small to medium onion, minced
⅓ ounce ginger, made into a paste, plus extra juliennes for garnish, optional
2 fat garlic cloves, made into a paste
¼ teaspoon ground turmeric
1 teaspoon ground coriander
Salt and ½ teaspoon freshly ground black pepper, or to taste (pitta please omit)
Generous 1 cup good-quality chicken stock
3 medium chicken breasts or 4 boned thighs, skinned and cut into large pieces
Generous 1 to 1¼ cups coconut milk
¾ teaspoon garam masala (pitta please omit)
2 to 2½ teaspoons lime or lemon juice
6½ to 7 ounces rice noodles (you can also use wheat), cooked according to package directions
7 ounces vegetables of your choice, blanched or steamed (I add three; choose from green beans, broccoli, snow peas, bean sprouts, bok choi)
Handful of mint and cilantro leaves and a little finely julienned carrot

Heat the oil in a medium nonstick saucepan. Add the onion and cook until soft and turning golden at the edges. Add the ginger and garlic pastes and cook for 40 to 50 seconds, stirring often until the garlic smells cooked. Add the spices, seasoning, and a small splash of water and cook until the water has evaporated and the paste has had 20 to 30 seconds to cook.

Add the stock, bring to a boil, and simmer, covered, for 12 minutes. The water should be quite reduced. Add the chicken, coconut milk, and garam masala, bring to a boil, then cover and simmer on low heat for 3 to 4 minutes for breast and 5 to 6 minutes for thigh (depending on how large the pieces are), or until the chicken is done. The curry should be of a medium creamy consistency. Stir in the lime or lemon juice, taste, and adjust the seasoning.

Place the cooked noodles in individual bowls or deep side plates, add the chicken on one side and the vegetables in neat piles on the other, and pour over the coconut curry. Garnish with lots of fresh mint and cilantro and carrot julienne.

# Hianese Chicken Rice

**VATA**
Great for vata

**PITTA**
Great for pitta

**KAPHA**
Great occasionally

This is such an unassuming dish but it is really flavorful. Chicken is poached in an aromatic broth and served on rice with a simple sauce and a few garnishes sprinkled over. It is one of Singapore's most famed dishes and luckily works with Ayurvedic principles. The chicken is grounding and nourishing and works for all doshas. It is not as complicated as it may seem but needs to be prepared in stages; it is well worth making.

**Serves 2**

2 small chicken breasts, skinned
To serve: chopped cucumber (vata and pitta), scallion (kapha), and cilantro (all)

**Poaching liquid**
5 cups good-quality chicken stock
2 scallions
4 large garlic cloves, lightly crushed
1-inch piece of ginger, sliced
10 black peppercorns

**Aromatic rice**
1 tablespoon vegetable oil
1 small to medium onion, minced
2 garlic cloves, chopped
Scant ⅔ cup jasmine or basmati rice, washed well and left to dry

**Ginger chile dressing**
½ small Chinese red chile, finely sliced
1½ teaspoons lemon juice
1 teaspoon rice vinegar
1 teaspoon sugar
Salt and freshly ground black pepper

**Soy dressing**
2 teaspoons light soy sauce
1 teaspoon unrefined sugar
12 drops of sesame oil
2 teaspoons vegetable oil
½ teaspoon dark soy sauce

Bring the ingredients for the poaching liquid to a boil in a saucepan that will contain the two chicken breasts snugly. Boil for 15 minutes to allow the flavors to infuse. Turn the heat to its lowest setting, add the chicken, and poach, uncovered, in barely simmering water for 10 to 12 minutes, depending on thickness. Take out and keep warm by wrapping in foil.

While the chicken is poaching, start the rice. Heat the oil in a small nonstick saucepan, add the onion, and cook until soft. Add the garlic and stir-fry for 40 seconds. Add the rice, stir well to coat in the oil, then take off the heat and wait for the chicken to finish cooking. When it is cooked, strain and set aside the chicken stock and, separately, set aside the cooked ginger and garlic (for the dressing).

Add generous 1 cup of the stock to the rice. Gently bring to a boil, then cover with a tight-fitting lid, turn the heat down, and simmer, undisturbed, for 10 to 12 minutes. Check a grain after 10 minutes; if it is not cooked through, return to the heat for another couple of minutes.

While the rice is cooking, grate the reserved cooked ginger and garlic on a microplane or fine grater and mix in the remaining ingredients for the ginger chile dressing, adding 2 tablespoons of the reserved chicken stock; season to taste.

Stir together the ingredients for the soy dressing, adding 3 tablespoons of the chicken stock.

To serve, divide the rice between two plates. Slice the chicken into fine strips on the diagonal, place on top of the rice, and spoon over the soy dressing (if using). Top with the appropriate garnishes and serve with the ginger chile dressing on the side.

# VEGETARIAN DISHES

Vegetables cover all the six tastes—sweet (potatoes, carrots), sour (tomatoes), salty (spinach, seaweed), bitter (endive), pungent (watercress), astringent (cauliflower)—so can provide all that our bodies need to function and be nourished. Add the protein of beans into the mix and you have a treasure trove of nutrients. If you are vegetarian, you will already know that you are able to look and feel fantastic on a balanced vegetarian diet.

This chapter is full of recipes inspired by ingredients that are good for the three doshas and cooked into easy-to-digest meals. There are some side dishes, but you can also scale down other recipes to serve on the side. Feel free to mix and match, as long as ingredients and cooking methods suit your dosha.

# One-Pot Lentil and Vegetable Curry

VATA
Use yellow mung lentils

PITTA
Omit chiles and pepper and add coconut

KAPHA
Great for kapha

This is a delicious lentil and vegetable curry that can bubble away in the kitchen but doesn't need too much attention. Soaking the lentils in advance will greatly reduce their cooking time. This is a good way for kapha and pitta to get their protein, but pitta should leave out the chiles and black pepper and can add 3 tablespoons of coconut milk or fresh grated coconut, which is cooling and will give it another layer of flavor. Vata can make it with yellow mung lentils as they would find it hard to digest the split beans (cooking time will be 30 to 35 minutes).

**Serves 4**

¾ cup Bengal gram (chana dal), washed well
4 cups water
1 pound seasonal vegetables, cut into small pieces (see the food charts on pages 153–158 for suitable examples)
¾ teaspoon ground turmeric
Salt
1 to 2 tablespoons ghee or vegetable oil (kapha 1 tablespoon, pitta 1½ tablespoons, vata 2 tablespoons)
Pinch of asafetida
¾ teaspoon mustard seeds
10 curry leaves
1 large shallot, chopped
1 fat garlic clove, minced

**Spice paste**
½ teaspoon ghee
¾ teaspoon cumin seeds
¾ teaspoon coriander seeds
1 dried red chile (kapha only)
5 black peppercorns (pitta omit)
½-inch cinnamon shard
1½ teaspoons Bengal gram (chana dal)

Place the lentils and water in a medium saucepan. Bring to a boil and skim off the scum that forms on the surface. Partially cover for 10 minutes, then cover and let simmer for 30 to 40 minutes, or until soft. Mash 3 tablespoons of the lentils, then stir back in. Add your vegetables to the pan with the turmeric and salt to taste. Simmer, covered, for 10 minutes, or until the vegetables are soft.

Meanwhile, heat the ghee for the spice paste in a small saucepan and roast all the ingredients until these have darkened to a nutty brown. Scrape into a sturdy mortar and pestle and grind to a fine powder.

Heat the tablespoon of ghee in a small pan and add the asafetida. When it sizzles, add the mustard seeds, and once they are popping add the curry leaves. After a minute add the shallot and cook until soft, then add the garlic. Cook for another 1 to 2 minutes, then add the roasted spice paste and cook for 10 seconds. Pour the mixture into the lentils and stir. The lentils should be a beautiful creamy mass. Serve with bread or rice.

# Vegetables and Edamame in Chile, Ginger Coconut Broth

VATA
Omit chile and pepper

PITTA
Omit chile and pepper

KAPHA
Great for kapha

This is a great dish for kapha. Edamame (soybeans) have a wonderful flavor and are high in protein; they can be found in the freezer section of supermarkets or health food stores (look for GMO-free). Use fava beans when in season or even half a package of firm tofu instead of the soybeans, or vary the vegetables. Even though there is coconut milk in this dish, the quantity is small and this type of lightly spiced brothy dish is really easy to digest and grounding. This dish can work for vata and even pitta without the chile and black pepper. Serve with basmati rice (vata and pitta) or add some cooked bean thread noodles (cellophane noodles) to the bottom of your bowl— they are made from mung beans, which are good for kapha.

**Serves 2**

1 tablespoon vegetable oil
10 black peppercorns (pitta omit)
1 small onion, sliced
1 Chinese red chile, stalks off (medium heat, more for flavor) (pitta omit)
½-ounce piece ginger, peeled weight
3 fat garlic cloves, peeled
1 lemongrass stalk, halved and bruised with a rolling pin, or a little lemon zest
Generous 1 cup water
Salt
1 small carrot, sliced thinly on the diagonal
3½ ounces small broccoli florets
1 head bok choy, quartered
⅓ cup coconut milk
⅔ cup edamame (soybeans) or fava beans, cooked (shelled weight)
1 to 1½ teaspoons lemon or lime juice
Cilantro leaves

Heat the vegetable oil in a medium nonstick pan, add the black peppercorns and onion, and sauté until soft and lightly golden.

Meanwhile, blend together three-quarters of the chile with the ginger and garlic and a splash of water to make a smooth paste. Add this to the cooked onions with the lemongrass. Reduce over moderate heat until you have only the paste, then cook over low heat for 3 to 4 minutes, or until little oil droplets appear around the pan.

Slice the remaining chile and add to the pan. Add the water and season. Add the carrots, cook for 5 minutes, then add the broccoli and bok choy, cover, and simmer for 4 to 5 minutes, or until they are just cooked. There should be enough water in the pan to do this, but if the pan starts to dry up, add a splash of water from the kettle.

Add the coconut milk, edamame beans, and lemon juice, bring back to a boil, and serve garnished with the cilantro.

# Risotto with Pumpkin Seed, Mint, and Fava Bean Pesto

**VATA**
Can add Parmesan and extra butter

**PITTA**
Great for pitta but omit salt and pepper

**KAPHA**
Omit the pesto

**Serves 2**

**Pesto**
1 tablespoon pumpkin seeds
Scant ¼ cup fava beans, blanched and shelled
2 teaspoons olive oil (vata can add an extra 2 teaspoons oil)
1 teaspoon water
2 tablespoons mint leaves

3⅓ to 3½ cups vegetable stock
1 teaspoon vegetable oil
1 rounded tablespoon butter or ghee (kapha use ¾ tablespoon)
2 small shallots, minced
1 large garlic clove, minced
¾ cup arborio rice
4 asparagus spears, sliced diagonally
¼ to ½ small zucchini, finely sliced
⅓ cup fava beans (2 cups in pods)
¼ small radicchio, finely shredded lengthwise
1 tablespoon each chopped mint, tarragon, basil, and dill, or other soft herbs
½ teaspoon fennel seeds, ground, optional
Salt and freshly ground black pepper (pitta omit)

With this risotto, everything cooks slowly in one pot, rendering it easier to digest. This is great for pitta and vata (vata can add Parmesan at the end); kapha should stick to small portions and leave out this pesto. Vata can also use normal pesto made with basil, pine nuts, and Parmesan.

Heat the stock in a pan; keep on low simmer. Heat the oil and butter in a large pan. Add the shallots and cook until soft. Add the garlic, cook for 30 seconds. Add the rice and stir for 2 minutes. Add a ladle of stock and stir. Cook on low heat, adding more stock once the last bit has been absorbed, stirring often. If you run out of stock, add hot water. After 18 minutes, add the vegetables and continue cooking for 4 to 5 minutes, or until the rice is cooked. The rice should be al dente and not stuck together.

Puree the pesto ingredients to make a coarse paste. Stir the herbs, fennel powder, seasoning, and a spoonful of the pesto into the rice.

**Opposite:** Risotto with Pumpkin Seed, Mint, and Fava Bean Pesto

# Pearl Barley Risotto

**VATA**
Eat in moderation

**PITTA**
Great for pitta

**KAPHA**
Great for kapha

**Vegetable options**
Add 2 ounces greens from list (see pages 153–158); stir in after 40 minutes
Add 3½ ounces broccoli, zucchini, peas, etc.; stir in as above with soft herbs
Butternut squash; roast 5 ounces with ½ sliced red onion and thyme; add at the end
Sauté 7 ounces mushrooms in oil, add 1 teaspoon chopped garlic, cook for 1 minute, add lemon juice and parsley

3 to 3⅓ cups vegetable stock
1 to 2 tablespoons vegetable oil or ghee (kapha 1 tablespoon oil)
½ medium onion, chopped
Handful of sliced leeks (white parts only)
2 thyme sprigs and 10 oregano leaves or rosemary, or soft herbs such as tarragon, parsley, basil, dill, or chives stirred in at the end
1 large garlic clove, chopped
½ cup pearl barley
Handful of arugula or watercress
1 to 2 tablespoons grated Parmesan cheese, optional
Salt and lots of freshly ground black pepper
Squeeze of lemon juice

**Serves 2**

Pearl barley is a wonderful ingredient for kapha and pitta and a nutritious, inexpensive grain. It does take a long time to cook and needs lots of added flavors, such as these vegetable options, to make it interesting. This grain is great for reducing swelling or water retention. It is also beneficial for vata as long as it is not consumed to excess. Omit the Parmesan if you have been eating more dairy than you should (this goes for kapha and pitta).

Heat the stock in a pan and keep it simmering gently. Heat the oil in a nonstick pan. Add the onion, leek, and stronger herbs; cook until the onion is soft. Add the garlic and cook for 1 minute. Add the barley and stir for 1 minute, then stir in a ladle of stock. Once absorbed, stir in the next, and continue this way until the pearl barley is cooked al dente. Add your veg option after 40 minutes, or if already cooked, stir into the finished dish with herbs or greens and Parmesan (if using). Season, add lemon juice.

# Winter Squash, Tofu, and Tamari Rice

VATA
Great for vata

PITTA
Great for pitta

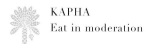

KAPHA
Eat in moderation

This is a rich rice and vegetable dish with some Japanese flavors. It is quite a nourishing dish and the Kabocha squash is delicious here, but can happily be substituted with butternut squash. This is a great dish for vata and pitta but a little heavy in terms of the sweet taste for kapha, but they can always serve small portions and supplement with vegetables. Vata can also serve smaller portions without the tofu and add some broiled salmon on the side.

**Serves 2 to 3, or 4 as a side dish**

Scant ½ cup white or brown rice
(I use basmati, but any will do),
washed
1 tablespoon vegetable oil
1 small onion, minced
2 teaspoons minced ginger
3 to 4 teaspoons tamari (wheat-free
soy sauce) or dark soy sauce
1 tablespoon raw cane sugar
1 tablespoon Japanese mirin
9 ounces Kabocha squash or butternut
squash, skin left on and cut
into ½-inch cubes
⅔ cup water
3½ ounces firm tofu, cut into ½-inch
cubes, or a handful of cooked
aduki beans
Generous ¾ cup peas, shelled weight
(or use frozen)
1 teaspoon black sesame seeds (vata)
or 2 teaspoons pumpkin seeds
(pitta), raw or lightly roasted

Cook and drain the rice according to package directions.

Heat the oil in a medium nonstick saucepan. Add the onion and cook until soft. Add the ginger, tamari, sugar, mirin, and let bubble for 1 minute, then add the squash with the water. Bring to a boil, cover, and simmer for 15 minutes, or until the squash is just soft. Add the tofu and peas after 5 minutes (if using frozen peas, add after 10 minutes).

When done, add the cooked rice and stir all together gently, cover and leave on very low heat for 4 to 5 minutes to allow the flavors to marry. Uncover and allow any excess water to cook off, leaving sweet, savory, and slightly sticky rice.

Serve sprinkled with the sesame seeds (vata) or pumpkin seeds (pitta).

# Ayurvedic Lentil Curry

**VATA**
Suits all doshas

**PITTA**
Suits all doshas

**KAPHA**
Suits all doshas

Lentils are one of the cornerstones of Ayurvedic food, especially yellow mung lentils, but these red lentils are equally easy to digest and both contain a high level of protein, which makes them a fantastic addition to your diet. When combined, they have a much better flavor. This dish is fantastic for all three doshas and is great when your system is feeling sluggish or if you have been eating too much animal protein. This curry is really easy to make and perfect Ayurvedic fare; serve with flat breads or rice, or kapha can also choose pearl barley and a vegetable from your list.

**Serves 4**

½ cup red lentils, washed
½ cup yellow mung lentils, washed
3½ cups water
¼ teaspoon ground turmeric
¼ cup chopped onion
2 fat garlic, cloves minced
⅓-ounce piece ginger, minced
1 to 2 green chiles, left whole (kapha only)
Salt
2 to 4 teaspoons ghee or vegetable oil (kapha 1 teaspoon oil; vata and pitta 2 to 3 teaspoons ghee)
1½ teaspoons cumin seeds
¼ teaspoon nigella seeds
1 teaspoon ground coriander
½ teaspoon garam masala (if you have a pitta imbalance, replace with ½ teaspoon ground fennel seeds)
Large handful of cilantro leaves, shredded
2 teaspoons lemon juice or to taste

Put the lentils and water in a saucepan and bring to a gentle simmer. Add the ground turmeric, onion, garlic, ginger, chiles, and salt and simmer for 30 minutes, or until soft and the red lentils are breaking down, giving the pan an occasional stir. Add more water to the pan at any time if it reduces too much.

Heat the ghee or oil in a small saucepan, add the seeds, and once they sizzle for 10 seconds or become aromatic, take off the heat and add the remaining spices. Pour the mixture into your cooked lentils and stir in the cilantro leaves. Taste and adjust the seasoning and add lemon juice to taste.

# Steamed Tofu with Vegetables and Soba Noodles

PITTA
Great for pitta; omit the chiles

KAPHA
Great for kapha

**Serves 2**

Tamari (wheat-free soy sauce) or soy sauce, to taste
3½ to 4 ounces (if hungry) soba or other noodles (wheat or rice noodles best for pitta)
Salt
Handful of broccoli, cut into florets
3¼ ounces sugar snap peas
11 ounces silken tofu or 7 ounces firm tofu

**Stock**
12 to 16 dried shiitake mushrooms (depending on size), well-rinsed
2 pieces of Kombu or wakame seaweed
3 garlic cloves, sliced
¾-ounce piece ginger, sliced
2 green scallions, chopped into 2-inch lengths
½ teaspoon sesame oil
1 teaspoon Japanese vinegar
1½ to 2 teaspoons miso soup paste or to taste
1¾ cups water

**Mint and chile dressing**
1 teaspoon vegetable oil
¾ teaspoon sesame seed oil
1 teaspoon sugar
1 teaspoon Japanese rice vinegar (for a strong pitta imbalance use lemon juice)
½ teaspoon ginger paste
2 teaspoons water
½ teaspoon minced Chinese red chile (pitta please omit)
2 heaping teaspoons shredded mint leaves

Soba noodles are Japanese buckwheat noodles. They are soft and, when served in this aromatic broth, absolutely delicious. This is a great healthy, low-fat dish for kapha. For pitta I would substitute with rice or egg noodles, leave out the raw scallions and chiles, and add a little extra mint and cilantro in with the noodles. This dish works really well with the silken tofu, but if you like more texture you can use firm tofu, broiled in the oven for 3 minutes each side. This dish is not for vata.

Place all the ingredients for the stock in a saucepan. Bring to a boil and simmer for 20 minutes, adding a splash of extra water to the pan if necessary. Cook until there is about ⅓ cup of liquid left in the pan; strain the liquid, keep the mushrooms and discard the rest. Add tamari to taste.

Meanwhile, cook the noodles according to package directions (mine take 5 minutes). Using a slotted spoon, lift the noodles out of the pan, then add salt and broccoli to the pan. and cook for 1 minute. Add the sugar snap peas and cook until both are crisp tender. Drain.

Stir together all the ingredients for the dressing except the mint; season to taste with tamari. Set aside.

Place the tofu whole onto a small plate and steam in a double steamer or other apparatus for 5 to 6 minutes, or until hot.

Reheat the stock if it has cooled, then ladle into bowls. Add the soba noodles. Place the mushrooms on one side and the vegetables on another. Slide the tofu into the remaining space. Stir the mint into the dressing and drizzle the tofu and vegetables with the dressing.

# Broiled Ricotta, Asparagus, and Herb Wrap

VATA
Quick and easy
meal

PITTA
Quick and easy
meal

**Makes 2**

⅔ cup ricotta cheese
2 to 3¼ ounces soft, well-flavored goat cheese (vata can add extra)
4 walnut halves, roughly chopped
8 black olives (not soaked in brine), washed and minced
Salt and freshly ground black pepper (vata only)
16 thin asparagus spears or 8 large ones, sliced diagonally, blanched for 1 minute
½ teaspoon vegetable oil
¾ teaspoon balsamic vinegar
2 flour tortillas
12 mint leaves
2 tablespoons chopped parsley

Ricotta is a neutral cheese and doesn't imbalance pitta, but it does need an injection of flavor so I have mixed it with a little goat cheese and added the cooling, calming mint, asparagus, olives, and balsamic vinegar (if you have a strong pitta imbalance you might be better omitting this). This is too dairy-heavy for those with a kapha imbalance as they are prone to mucus which dairy exacerbates.

Beat together the ricotta, goat cheese, and walnuts. Add the olives and seasoning.

Heat the griddle or grill pan until hot. Toss the asparagus in the oil and season. Turn the griddle or pan heat to medium, add the asparagus, and cook for 2 to 3 minutes, without moving too much so that the asparagus is well marked. Toss in a bowl with the balsamic vinegar.

Spread half the cheese mixture in the middle of each tortilla. Top with the asparagus and herbs. Fold in all sides to enclose the filling. Place on the griddle or pan, seam side down, for 2 minutes, or until crisp. Turn over and repeat on the other side. Serve hot.

**Opposite:** Red Onion, Radicchio, and Goat Cheese Pizza

# Red Onion, Radicchio, and Goat Cheese Pizza

VATA
Good for vata

PITTA
Good for pitta
occasionally

KAPHA
Great for kapha;
choose corn tortillas

**Serves 2**

1 tablespoon vegetable oil
1 medium to large red onion, sliced
1 large garlic clove, chopped
½ radicchio, shredded
2 teaspoons balsamic vinegar
¼ teaspoon ground fennel seeds, optional
Salt and lots of freshly ground black pepper
2 flour (or corn) tortillas
½ ounce watercress leaves
1½ to 2 ounces soft well-flavored goat cheese, crumbled

A great kapha meal, with low-fat, pungent onions and bitter radicchio (you could also use endive or chicory). The pizza base is as light as a feather and the whole meal is satisfying. Those with a kapha imbalance are generally discouraged from having dairy but I don't believe any of us could give up an entire food group, so choose goat cheese as it is easier to digest than cow's milk. This pizza makes a great packed lunch if rolled into a wrap. This is also a great vata dish as cooked onions are good for them, although they can halve the amount of radicchio and add a little extra oil and cheese. This is also a good dish for pitta.

Heat the oil in a nonstick pan, add the onion, and cook for 8 minutes, or until caramelized. Add the garlic and cook for 1 minute. Add the radicchio and cook until wilted. Stir in the vinegar and fennel seeds, season, and cook for another minute.

Using tongs, hold one flour tortilla over an open flame for 1 minute, moving often and flipping sides so it doesn't burn. It will start to crisp up at the edges. Place on a plate, and repeat with the second tortilla. Spread the onions evenly over each tortilla, top with the watercress, and scatter with goat cheese. Serve immediately, or if you wish, place the pizza in the oven to warm the goat cheese.

# Coconut-Laced Spiced Spinach

VATA
Good for vata

PITTA
Good for pitta
occasionally

KAPHA
Great for kapha

**Serves 2**

1 shallot, quartered
1 largish garlic clove
2 to 4 teaspoons vegetable oil or ghee (kapha 2 teaspoons; pitta 3 teaspoons; vata 4 teaspoons)
¼ teaspoon mustard seeds (pitta please omit)
¼ teaspoon cumin seeds
⅛ teaspoon nigella seeds
1 dried red chile (only for kapha)
7 ounces spinach, shredded
Salt
2 to 4 teaspoons dry unsweetened coconut (kapha 2 teaspoons; pitta and vata 4 teaspoons)
½ teaspoon lemon juice or to taste

Spinach is a great vegetable for kapha and although it is mildly heating, it is actually fine for those with a pitta imbalance when eaten as part of a balanced diet. It is also great for vata (but if you have joint problems, the acidity in the spinach may aggravate them). It is amazing for cleansing the blood and is great for easing a dry cough, cold, or fever. Pitta should leave out some of the stronger spices (see above).

Puree the shallots with the garlic to a fine paste, adding a little water to help.

Heat the oil in a medium saucepan. Add the seeds, once they are popping properly turn the heat down and add the red chile (if using). Follow with the spinach, pureed shallots, and seasoning. Cook for 5 to 6 minutes over moderate heat or until all the excess water released by the spinach has dried off (this gives the shallot and garlic time to cook). Stir in the coconut and lemon juice to taste and serve.

# Sautéed Corn with Peppers

VATA
Good for vata

PITTA
Suits pitta

KAPHA
Good for balanced kapha

**Serves 2 to 3**

2 to 4 teaspoons vegetable oil, ghee, or butter (kapha 2 teaspoons oil; vata 3 teaspoons; pitta 4 teaspoons oil, ghee, or butter)
1 small onion, minced
½ large red bell pepper, chopped into ½-inch pieces
2 small ears of corn, kernels cut off with a knife
1 green chile, pierced with the tip of a knife (pitta avoid)
2 small garlic cloves, peeled, left whole but crushed to release the flavor
Salt and freshly ground black pepper
½ teaspoon ground cumin
¾ to 1 teaspoon lemon juice
Handful of cilantro leaves, chopped

This dish is good for those with a vata body type and those who are a balanced kapha (corn is quite sweet so should be eaten in moderation if you are overweight). Corn also suits pitta as it is sweet and cool. The onions and peppers add a wonderful, almost Mexican flavor to the dish and lighten the sweet starchiness of the corn. A great side dish for all.

Heat the oil in a medium nonstick saucepan. Add the onion, corn, pepper, chile, garlic, and salt. Sauté the vegetables over moderate heat, stirring often, for 8 minutes, or until they are soft, adding a small splash of water after 4 to 5 minutes.

Once cooked, add the ground cumin and lemon juice to taste, then adjust the seasoning and stir in the cilantro leaves. Remove the garlic and chile and serve.

# Southern-Style Sautéed Sweet Potatoes

VATA
Great for vata

PITTA
Great for pitta

**Serves 2 to 3**

1 tablespoon vegetable oil
    or ghee
½ teaspoon mustard seeds
    (pitta please omit)
¼ teaspoon nigella seeds
8 large curry leaves
1 rounded teaspoon
    minced ginger
1 small onion, minced
Salt and freshly ground
    black pepper
1 medium orange-fleshed
    sweet potato
    (14 ounces), diced
    into 1½-inch cubes
⅓ teaspoon ground fennel
    seed
1 teaspoon lemon juice

Sweet potatoes are easier to digest than normal potatoes and their sweet starchiness is great for vata and also pitta. I have always found them too sweet but here with some spices and savory elements it is quite delicious. Serve with Ayurvedic lentils or baked or roasted chicken.

Heat the oil in a wide nonstick saucepan. Add the mustard and nigella seeds and once they pop, add the curry leaves. Follow immediately with the ginger, onion, and salt. Cook over moderate heat until the onions are lightly golden at the edges.

Add the sweet potatoes and ground fennel seed and mix well. Pour in enough water to come one-third of the way up the vegetables. Bring to a boil, reduce the heat to moderate, cover, and cook for 12 to 14 minutes, or until the point of a knife goes easily through the vegetables.

When cooked, uncover—the water should all have been absorbed, but if not, dry off over high heat (do not stir at this point). Adjust the seasoning and add lime juice to taste.

# Savoy Cabbage with Peas

PITTA
Great for pitta

KAPHA
Great for kapha

**Serves 2 generously**

2 teaspoons vegetable oil
    or ghee
½ teaspoon cumin seeds
½ medium onion, minced
Salt
1 garlic clove, chopped
1 teaspoon chopped ginger
¼ teaspoon ground turmeric
½ teaspoon ground
    coriander
½ small head of savoy
    cabbage, finely shredded
Scant ⅔ cup green peas
    (fresh is preferable but
    frozen work well too)
1 tablespoon dry
    unsweetened coconut,
    optional for pitta; kapha
    please omit

Cabbage is a great vegetable for kapha and pitta to include in their diets. It is cooling, astringent, and bitter—all fantastic elements for these two doshas. I prefer the taste of savoy cabbage to the more usual white cabbage, which seems to lack flavor; even Chinese cabbage is a better option. Those with a pitta imbalance are advised to avoid spices so often feel their diet is quite limited, so try this simple Indian side that goes really well with the Ayurvedic lentils and some rice or Indian breads.

Heat the oil in a large nonstick saucepan. Add the cumin seeds and once they become aromatic, add the onion and salt and cook until soft. Add the garlic and ginger, cook for 40 to 50 seconds, then add the ground spices and a good splash of water.

Follow with the cabbage and peas and cook gently for 5 to 6 minutes, or until the cabbage is wilted and the peas are cooked. Stir in the coconut (if using) and serve.

# Zucchini, Basil, and Goat Cheese Carbonara

VATA
Great for vata

PITTA
Eat only
occasionally

KAPHA
Use buckwheat pasta
and less cheese

**Serves 2**

4½ ounces penne or
  rigatoni pasta
1 tablespoon olive oil
1 fat garlic clove, minced
½ medium onion, finely
  sliced
1 zucchini, very finely sliced
12 large basil leaves, half
  left whole, half shredded
2½ ounces goat cheese
  (weight without rind)
  or 1 ounce Parmesan
  cheese, grated
¼ teaspoon lemon zest
Squeeze of lemon juice
1 egg yolk
Salt and freshly ground
  black pepper

Traditional carbonara does not contain cream and is much lighter than recent versions of the dish. Carbonara should get its creaminess from an egg yolk and Parmesan. I have used goat cheese as it is easier to digest, but you can opt for the Parmesan. This unctuous pasta dish is ideal for vata, but also okay for pitta occasionally (they should limit their intake of sour, salty cheeses). Kapha can enjoy it sometimes as it is quite light (but use buckwheat pasta which is a healthier option for you and add less cheese).

Bring a large pan of water to a boil. Season with salt and add the pasta, cook until al dente.

Meanwhile, put the oil and garlic in a wide nonstick pan and heat gently. Once the garlic has been gently sizzling for 1 minute, add the onion, zucchini, whole basil leaves, and a little salt, stir well to mix, cover, and cook very gently for 5 to 7 minutes, or until the zucchini are soft (depends on their thickness).

Set aside 2 to 3 tablespoons of the cooking water. Drain the pasta, add to the zucchini with the reserved water, and mix well. Turn off the heat, add the goat cheese, basil, lemon zest and juice, and then the yolk. Stir immediately so the yolk coats everything (it will cook in the residual heat) and season.

# Cannellini Beans with Kale

VATA
Eat only
occasionally

PITTA
Reduce tomatoes
and add lemon juice

KAPHA
For kapha imbalance,
serve with polenta

**Serves 4, can easily
be halved**

1½ to 2 tablespoons olive oil
  (pitta 2 tablespoons)
2 large thyme sprigs
½ onion, chopped
¾ carrot, chopped
½ small leek, white part only,
  halved lengthwise and
  sliced
2 garlic cloves, minced
1 medium to large tomato,
  skinned and pureed
½ teaspoon ground cumin
½ teaspoon vegetable
  bouillon powder
  or to taste, mixed into
  ¾ cup water
1 dried red chile (kapha only)
3¼ ounces curly kale,
  shredded
14-ounce can cannellini
  beans, rinsed, or 1 cup
  dried (see pages 56–57)
Salt and freshly ground black
  pepper (kapha only)

With their fiber, astringency, and protein, these beans are great for kapha and pitta. Kale is a balancing green for both these doshas, is rich in minerals and vitamins and a natural blood cleanser. For a kapha imbalance, try it with Salt and Pepper Herb Polenta (see page 140). For a strong pitta imbalance, use half the amount of tomato, sharpen with lemon juice at the end, and serve with bread, rice, or quinoa. You can also use cranberry, pinto, or navy beans.

Heat the oil in a medium nonstick pan. Add the thyme, onion, carrot, and leek and sauté gently until the onion is soft. Add the garlic and cook, stirring, for 1 minute. Add the tomato, ground cumin, and three-quarters of the stock, bring to a boil, and simmer gently for 15 minutes, or until completely reduced.

Add the kale and a splash of the stock and cook for 5 minutes. Add the beans, another splash of stock, and cook for another 5 minutes, or until the mixture comes together. Taste and season (kapha can add pepper). The final dish should be loose (but I sometimes crush a handful of beans in the pan to thicken the sauce).

**Opposite:** Zucchini, Basil, and Goat Cheese Carbonara

# GRAINS

In this chapter you'll find grain-based recipes to pair with dishes in other chapters or to accompany meals you already cook at home. I wish I had enough space to include many more recipes, but hopefully these will get you started. Also, you can use sides from other recipes or even complete recipes, scaled down to make a side dish portion. Feel free to mix and match, as long as the ingredients suit your body type and you cook it in a way that is good for your dosha.

# Spelt Rotis

VATA
Great for vata

PITTA
Great for pitta

KAPHA
Eat only
occasionally

North Indians eat whole wheat flat breads with most meals. These are yeast-free which suits vata, and spelt is lower in gluten than wheat, which is good for all doshas (gluten increases mucus). I use half whole wheat and half spelt flour as together they make softer breads, but use whichever you prefer. There is no real skill involved—you just need a rolling pin. Don't worry about trying to make them into a perfect circle (although practice does make perfect)—make them whatever shape you like. Great for vata and pitta, also fine for kapha on the odd occasion.

**Makes 4, can easily be doubled**

½ cup whole wheat spelt flour (or half whole wheat and half white spelt flour), plus extra for dusting
⅓ cup water

Place the flour in a large bowl, add the water and, using your hands, mix the dough together. If you feel the dough is a little dry, add another teaspoon of water or so. Knead well for 4 to 5 minutes, or until the dough is smooth—the resulting dough will be just slightly sticky. Place in a bowl, cover with a damp dishtowel, and leave for 20 to 30 minutes to rest.

Divide the dough into four balls. Sprinkle your counter with a little extra flour. Take a ball in your palms, make a round shape, and then flatten it a little. Dip both sides in some extra flour and roll into a thin circle, 5 to 6 inches in diameter. The best way of doing this is to keep turning the dough a quarter circle as you roll.

Heat a tava (Indian flat griddle pan) or nonstick skillet until quite hot. Brush off excess flour and place the bread on the tava. Reduce heat to moderate and cook for 20 to 30 seconds, or until small bubbles appear on the underside, then turn and cook until the base has brown spots.

At this stage you can turn the roti and cook on the underside again until brown spots appear, but if you have a gas stove, you can try to get them to puff up. Place the roti (undercooked side facing the flame) directly over the flame using tongs and it will start to puff up. Keep it moving, allowing the bread to rest on the flame for no more than a second. The whole process takes only 5 to 6 seconds. Place on a plate. If you have an electric stove, press down gently on different areas of the cooked bread in the pan—as you press one area, the rest should puff up, then tackle the next area. Keep the bread warm by wrapping in a napkin or foil and keep in a low oven while you make the rest.

# Simple Rice Pilaf

VATA
Great for vata

PITTA
Omit the
peppercorns

KAPHA
Eat only occasionally,
ideally with quinoa

**Serves 4**

1 to 2 tablespoons ghee
or vegetable oil (kapha
1 tablespoon oil;
pitta 1½ tablespoons;
vata 2 tablespoons)
1 teaspoon cumin seeds
3 cloves (those with a
strong pitta imbalance
can avoid)
6 whole peppercorns
(pitta please omit)
1-inch cinnamon shard
1 small onion, thinly sliced
1 cup green peas, fresh or
frozen (fresh is better)
1 cup basmati rice (or
1½ cups quinoa),
cooked according to
package directions
½ teaspoon garam masala
1 tablespoon lemon juice
or to taste
Salt

This pilaf, shown with the soup on page 81, can be made with brown or white basmati rice or with quinoa (which suits kapha better). Ayurveda considers basmati rice to be superior to the other varieties of rice, and I find it very light and easy to digest. This is a really simple dish with lots of flavor but no strong spices, so perfect for the whole family to enjoy with any Indian dish.

Heat the ghee or oil in a large nonstick saucepan. Add the whole spices and cook for about 30 seconds. Add the onion and sauté gently for 6 minutes, or until lightly caramelized. Add the peas (if fresh) and a splash of water and cook, covered, for 7 to 8 minutes, or until cooked.

Add the rice (or quinoa), peas (if frozen), garam masala, lemon juice, salt, and a splash of water if the rice/quinoa is dry; gently stir-fry to heat through and serve.

**Opposite:** Quinoa with Roasted Vegetables and Chickpeas

# Quinoa with Roasted Vegetables and Chickpeas

VATA
Omit the chickpeas
and raisins

PITTA
Good for pitta

KAPHA
Omit the pine nuts

**Serves 2 as a main course, 3 to 4 as a side**

3 large asparagus spears,
sliced into ¾-inch pieces
½ zucchini, sliced into
half-moon shapes
1 small red onion, sliced
1 to 2 tablespoons olive oil
(kapha 1 tablespoon,
pitta 1½ tablespoons,
vata 2 tablespoons)
2 thyme sprigs
Salt and freshly ground
black pepper
½ cup quinoa, rinsed
1¼ tablespoons lemon juice
2 teaspoons raisins
(optional, not for vata)
1 tablespoon pine nuts,
lightly toasted (not
for kapha)
⅔ cup cooked chickpeas,
washed (vata replace
with cooked chicken or
feta/goat cheese)
¾ teaspoon ground cumin
Handful of parsley

Quinoa is a whole grain that has the highest amount of complete protein of any grain, making it invaluable in a vegetarian diet. It is light on the digestive system and suits everyone. This dish is a complete meal as quinoa has so much protein, but it can also be served as a side dish with chicken or fish (in which case leave out chickpeas). Can also be made with couscous or barley couscous

Preheat the oven to 400°F. In a roasting pan, toss the vegetables with the oil and thyme and season. Place on the middle shelf in the oven and roast for 15 to 20 minutes, or until soft.

Meanwhile, cook the quinoa according to the package directions in stock or water. It will have slightly burst and be just soft. Drain well.

Once the vegetables are done, spoon the cooked quinoa into the roasting pan. Add the lemon juice, raisins, pine nuts, extra drizzle of oil, chickpeas, cumin, and chopped parsley. Stir well and adjust seasoning.

# Griddled Herbed Flat Breads

VATA
Great for vata

PITTA
Great for pitta

KAPHA
Eat only
occasionally

**Makes 4 small breads**

1 teaspoon dried yeast
⅓ cup lukewarm water
1 cup white flour, or half white, half whole wheat spelt flour, plus extra for rolling out
¼ teaspoon salt
Handful of mint, parsley, or cilantro, chopped
Pinch of sugar
¼ teaspoon nigella seeds or fennel seeds, optional
2 teaspoons olive oil, plus extra for brushing

These wonderful soft breads work with many different flavors. They are quick to make but need to rise for at least an hour. You can use normal flour, but do try spelt flour as it works wonderfully and has a lower gluten content than normal flour. Serve with the meze platter (see page 87) or make small portions and serve with the soups for a light meal. Great for vata and pitta, but wheat should be kept to a minimum by kapha.

Mix the yeast with the water in a large bowl and let it dissolve. Mix the dry ingredients together and add to the yeast with the oil. Bring together into a dough, then transfer to a floured counter and knead to a soft dough, using extra flour if the dough is too sticky. Shape into a ball, place on a baking sheet and smear the surface with a little oil. Cover with a dishtowel and let rise in a warm place for 1 to 1½ hours, or until doubled in size. Knead in the herbs (if using).

Heat a griddle pan or stovetop grill pan until quite hot. Divide the dough into four. Flour your counter and roll out the dough into long flat breads—I like mine quite thin and they will puff up on the griddle. Lay on the griddle two at a time and brush with olive oil (optional). Cook over moderate heat for 2 to 3 minutes (depends on thickness of the dough), or until you have brown lines on the underside, flip over, and repeat on the other side. Repeat with the remaining dough.

# Salt and Pepper Herb Polenta

KAPHA
Perfect for kapha

**Serves 2 to 4 (2 if served soft, 4 if broiled and cut into wedges)**

2 teaspoons ghee/butter (a treat as it goes well with the polenta)
½ small onion, chopped
2 thyme sprigs, leaves only
1 good teaspoon shredded oregano leaves
1 small garlic clove, minced
2 cups good-quality vegetable stock (I use about ½ teaspoon vegetable bouillon powder)
⅛ teaspoon coarsely ground black pepper
Salt to taste
⅔ cup cornmeal

Cornmeal is a fantastic grain for kapha as it is quite drying, but many polenta dishes are laden down with cheese for flavor. I have used ghee as it does require some degree of richness. I often let it set on a plate, cut it into wedges, and broil (see below). Serve with Cannellini Beans with Kale (see page 134) or eat broiled wedges with soup or to supplement a salad. Ring the changes with some shredded sautéed cabbage, sauté diced red bell pepper with the onions, or add a handful of corn and a little pure ground chile and cumin powder.

Heat the ghee or butter in a medium nonstick pan. Add the onion and cook until soft and browning at the edges. Add the herbs and garlic and cook over low heat for 1 minute. Add the stock, bring to a boil, and simmer, covered, for 2 minutes. Season, then add the cornmeal while stirring. Increase the heat to medium and cook, stirring constantly, for 5 to 6 minutes, or until the cornmeal leaves the sides of the pan.

**For set polenta**
Cook a little more until it is quite thick, then pour out onto a small round plate. It usually settles into a nice round shape, ideally around 1 inch thick. Let set and broil or griddle before serving.

# Spinach and Onion Flat Breads

**VATA**
Fine for vata

**PITTA**
Omit the stronger spices

**KAPHA**
Perfect for kapha

These delicious breads are fantastic eaten with lentil or bean curry. They are full of flavor and the dough is really quick and easy to make. The breads themselves take just a minute a piece. The only caveat here is that the dough must be made just before cooking, otherwise the spinach will continue to release moisture and the dough will become too sticky. You can make them in advance and reheat in some foil in the oven. These breads are fantastic for kapha as the spinach and addition of gram flour lightens them and reduces the amount of gluten, which really doesn't suit kapha. The onions add extra flavor but are optional. These breads can also be enjoyed by the other two doshas, but pitta should leave out the stronger spices, see below.

**Makes 4 small breads**

⅓ cup chapati flour (mix of whole wheat and all-purpose, or use just one), plus extra for rolling out
¼ cup gram flour
¼ teaspoon cumin seeds
⅛ teaspoon ajowan seeds (pitta please leave out)
Pinch of pure ground chile powder (kapha only)
Scant ¼ teaspoon salt
2½ ounces spinach leaves, washed, water squeezed out and minced
1 rounded tablespoon chopped onion or shallot (pitta please omit)
1 tablespoon yogurt
1 to 2 tablespoons vegetable oil (vata 2 tablespoons, pitta, 2 tablespoons, kapha 1 tablespoon)

In a large bowl, stir together the dry ingredients. Add the spinach, onion, yogurt, and oil and mix well with your hands—the more you squeeze and knead the dough, the more water the spinach releases and binds the dough.

Heat a tava (Indian flat griddle pan) or nonstick skillet until quite hot.

Divide the dough into four equal-sized balls. Flatten the first ball with the heel of your hand and dip both sides in extra flour and roll out to make a circle 4 inches in diameter. It won't roll into a perfect circle so please don't worry!

Slap the bread onto the hot surface. Cook for 10 seconds, then flip the bread over. Turn the heat down to a medium–low setting. Drizzle ¼ teaspoon (½ teaspoon for vata) of the remaining oil over the bread, and spread with the back of the spoon. Keep moving the bread in the pan so that no single area gets all the heat. Turn over again and cook for another 10 seconds, drizzling another ¼ teaspoon (½ teaspoon for vata) of oil over the bread. It should be tinged with brown spots.

Keep the cooked bread warm, covered in foil, and repeat with the rest of the dough.

# DESSERTS

We are predisposed to enjoy sweetness
and it is the most nourishing of all tastes,
but in Ayurveda "sweet" refers to the
inherent sweetness in foods, not sugary
products. While desserts, as such, are not
advocated in Ayurveda (our body digests
the sweet tastes first and eating a large
amount at the end of a meal will put a lot
of pressure on our digestive systems), it is
a hard habit to break and if it is good for the
soul, it is good for us (in moderation). Also,
we tend to eat dessert after having eaten
a full meal which just means we overeat, again
burdening our agni. If you plan on having
dessert, eat a little less main course and try
not to eat a large portion by yourself—
share with a friend. My dessert portions
are deliberately small so that you can enjoy
them without feeling too heavy or guilty.

Fresh fruit should be eaten
separately from meals, but cooking
fruit changes its nature somewhat
and it does not clash with food
making it a better dessert
options. Fruit and dairy can
be a hard combination to
digest and if you find
yourself bloated after this
combination, avoid it in the future.

If you are vata, opt for warming, comforting desserts. For a pitta
imbalance, choose desserts, which are cooling and contain dairy
or coconut, but avoid too many sour fruits, crème fraîche, and icy
desserts. If you are kapha, stick to lighter, fruit-based dishes.

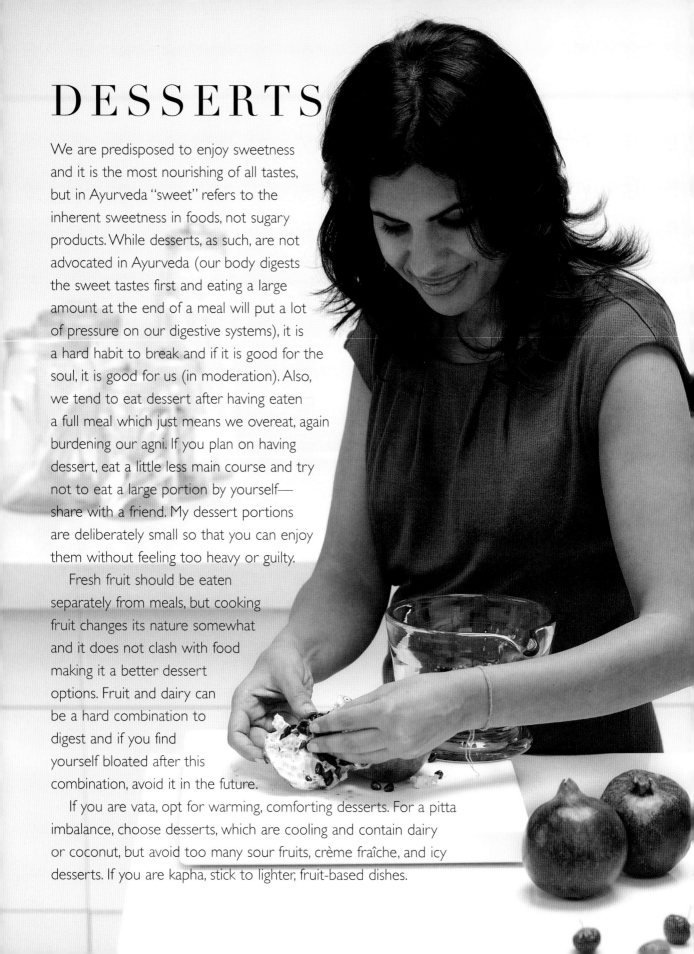

# Cooling Coconut and Lemon Cupcakes

VATA
Fine for vata

PITTA
Good for pitta

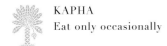

KAPHA
Eat only occasionally

I have always loved cupcakes (who doesn't?) and make often them with my daughter and her friends. These cupcakes are cooling on the body (and therefore suitable for pitta) as I have not used heating egg yolks and, instead, have added cooling milk and coconut to the mix. The lemon zest adds a wonderful contrast to the coconut, but you could also add orange zest or leave it out altogether. There are so many twists to the basic cupcake—try omitting the coconut and adding more lemon and a tablespoon of black poppy seeds or a handful of blueberries. They are light and fluffy, and you won't miss the yolks. Also good for vata and okay for kapha on the odd occasion.

**Makes 6 cupcakes; can easily be doubled**

¾ cup all-purpose flour
Small pinch of salt
¾ teaspoon baking powder
3 tablespoons butter, soft and at room
    temperature
¼ cup raw cane sugar
1 large egg white
5 tablespoons milk
½ teaspoon vanilla extract
½ teaspoon lemon zest
¼ cup dry unsweetened coconut

**Frosting**
¼ cup confectioners' sugar
1 to 1½ teaspoons milk
2 tablespoons flaked, toasted, or
    dry unsweetened coconut, or
    slivered, toasted almonds (for vata)

Preheat the oven to 350°F. Line a muffin pan with six cupcake papers.

Stir together the flour, salt, and baking powder.

Whisk together the butter and sugar until really soft and creamy. Add the egg white and whisk until well incorporated. Add one-third of the milk along with the vanilla extract and whisk in thoroughly.

Add about one-third of the flour mixture and stir in gently but thoroughly, using a spoon or spatula. Stir in half the remaining milk, then the half the remaining flour mixture and repeat with last batch. Stir in the lemon zest and coconut.

Spoon the batter into the cupcake papers so that they are nearly full. Place in the middle of the oven and bake for 18 to 22 minutes, or until a toothpick inserted in the center comes out clean. Let cool in the pan for 10 minutes.

When the cupcakes have cooled, mix together the confectioners' sugar and milk. Spread a thin film over the top of the cupcakes using the back of a small spoon and sprinkle abundantly with the coconut or slivered almonds. Enjoy!

# Strawberry and Pomegranate Shortcake

VATA
Good for vata

PITTA
May use blueberries
instead of strawberries

This recipe is based on the American shortcake dessert which is somewhere between a scone and a cookie and has a wonderful texture. My version is not as rich, but the strawberries and their liquor add a delicious moistness. I cook the strawberries a little to make them easier to digest with the cake and cream. This is a refreshing treat and perfect for a vata imbalance. For a pitta imbalance, use blueberries instead of strawberries.

**Makes 1 large cake or 8 small individual ones**

2 cups all-purpose flour
1 tablespoon baking powder
4 tablespoons raw cane or raw
    brown sugar
¼ teaspoon salt
4 tablespoons cold butter, cut into
    small cubes
1 egg, well beaten
⅓ cup cold milk, set aside 1 teaspoon
    to brush over cake
¾ teaspoon vanilla extract
Scant ⅔ cup heavy cream
Confectioners' sugar

**Strawberry and pomegranate compote**
Juice of 1 orange
4 tablespoons water
¼ cup sugar
1 star anise (optional but delicious)
1 vanilla bean or ½ teaspoon vanilla
    extract
2¾ cups strawberries, hulled and
    quartered(use blueberries
    for a pitta imbalance)
Fruit of ½ sweet pomegranate
    (optional)

To make the compote, heat the orange juice, water, sugar, star anise, and scraped vanilla bean or extract in a pan. Simmer until the sugar has melted, then boil for 2 minutes. Add the strawberries and cook for another 2 minutes, or until the fruit soften. Turn off the heat and add the pomegranate fruit. Let cool.

Preheat the oven to 425°F. Grease and flour an 8-inch round cake pan or a cookie sheet for individual cakes.

Mix the flour, baking powder, sugar, and salt in a large bowl. Rub the butter into the dry ingredients with your fingertips until the flour looks like fine sand. Whisk together the egg, milk, and vanilla extract and pour into a well in the middle of the dry ingredients. Stir, drawing in the flour from the sides. Gather together with your hands and give it the lightest knead just to bring it together—it might need only four or five turns. Place in the cake pan and press down, or pat into a square, cut into 8 pieces, press each piece into a circle, and place on cookie sheet. Bake for 15 to 17 minutes for single portions and 20 to 25 minutes for the larger cake, or until a toothpick comes out clean. Take out of the oven and cool. Then, using a serrated knife, halve the cake(s) horizontally.

Whip the cream until it forms soft peaks. Remove the star anise and vanilla bean, if using, from the compote. Spread the cream over the base of the cake(s) and spoon the strawberries and juices on top. Add the upper layer of the cake(s). Dust with confectioners' sugar and serve.

**Lower fat version**
Omit the cream and serve with the fruit and juices—it is still delicious. Alternatively, whisk 1 cup fresh ricotta cheese with 1 tablespoon of honey and a little of the juices to make a whipped cream consistency.

# Baked Spice-Stuffed Apples

VATA
Serve with sour cream

PITTA
Serve with ice cream

KAPHA
Good for kapha

**Makes 1; can be increased to serve more**

1 sweet apple, peeled and rubbed with lemon juice
1 rounded teaspoon raw brown or cane sugar
¼ cup nuts, roughly chopped (I like to use walnuts, almonds, and roasted hazelnuts)
¼ teaspoon ground cinnamon
Pinch of grated nutmeg
1 rounded teaspoon raisins or other dried fruit
Scant ⅓ cup apple juice
1½ teaspoons butter

Cooked apples are very good to perk up our ojas (our vitality), so it is good to include them in our diet. This dessert is ideal for those with a kapha imbalance and it should ideally be eaten as it is on its own, but vata can eat it with a little sour cream or crème fraîche on the side and pitta can drizzle over a little cream.

Preheat the oven to 375°F. Core the apple to make a neat hole 1 inch in diameter. Slice off the base of the apple so it can stand upright.

Mix together the sugar, nuts, cinnamon, nutmeg, and raisins. Pack into the cavity of the apple. Place in a snug fitting baking dish and pour around the apple juice. Top the apple with the butter. Cover with foil and bake for 8 minutes. Remove foil and continue cooking the apple until soft, basting every 6 to 7 minutes or so; this takes 40 to 45 minutes.

**In a hurry?**
For a quicker dish, cut the apples in half and core, then cook in their skins for 25 minutes.

**Proper Ayurveda**
Eat the apples without any dairy products. Ideally kapha can make the quick version (see above), omit the sugar and drizzle honey over at the end.

**Opposite:** Baked Spice-Stuffed Apples

# Almond, Orange, and Fennel Seed Biscotti

VATA
Suits all doshas

PITTA
Suits all doshas

KAPHA
Suits all doshas

**Makes approx 30 small pieces; quantities can be halved**

1 egg and 1 egg white
½ cup raw cane or turbinado sugar (a coarse, raw sugar)
1 teaspoon vanilla extract
½ teaspoon almond extract
1 tablespoon butter, melted
Scant 1 cup whole almonds, chopped coarsely (can substitute with other nuts or seeds)
¾ teaspoon baking powder
1¾ cups all-purpose flour
Zest of 1 orange
1½ teaspoons fennel seeds
1 teaspoon ground cinnamon

An almost fat-free cookie that is perfect with tea or coffee or as a little something sweet after a meal. The biscotti are twice baked and therefore crunchier than normal cookies, which makes them so satisfying. The fennel seed aids digestion and cleanses your breath, so is a good way to end the meal. They suit all doshas, but vata and kapha spice-lovers can add a few black peppercorns (½ teaspoon cooked in the butter for 40 seconds)—I love their punch of flavor and they further aid digestion.

Preheat the oven to 350°F. Line a cookie sheet with wax paper or brush with oil.

Lightly whisk together the eggs and sugar in a large bowl. Add the vanilla and almond extract and melted butter. Mix together the remaining dry ingredients and stir into the eggs, to give a slightly soft dough. Divide into two and shape each into a log, about 2 inches wide and 1 inch high. Place on the cookie sheet and bake for 25 minutes, or until firm and lightly golden.

Cool a little, then slice on the diagonal into pieces ½ inch thick. Place the slices back on the cookie sheet, cut side up. Cook for another 15 to 18 minutes, or until lightly golden, turning halfway. Let cool, then store in an airtight container.

# Saffron and Cardamom Rice Creams

VATA
Great for vata

PITTA
Great for pitta

KAPHA
Eat occasionally

This is a light, Indian comfort dessert that is really easy to digest and cooling on the stomach. The saffron balances all the doshas and the cardamom adds just a little warmth. It is a great dessert for vata and pitta and is a good option for the occasional dessert for kapha, too, as it is quite healthy. I prefer to serve these as they are, without any fruit garnish which would make them harder to digest, but when you have people around and still want to stick to a healthy diet, try serving with poached dried figs or even fresh figs drizzled with honey.

**Makes 4 small portions**

2½ tablespoons rice flour
2 tablespoons sugar
1 tablespoon ground almonds
2 cups whole milk
Good pinch of saffron threads
2 green cardamom pods, husks
    removed and seeds ground
Caramelized rose almonds or
    2 teaspoons lightly toasted
    slivered almonds

In a bowl, mix the rice flour, sugar, and ground almonds together with 5 tablespoons of the milk to make a smooth paste.

Heat the remaining milk with the saffron in a saucepan over medium heat, stirring constantly. As you bring it up to a simmer, stir in the milk and rice flour mixture.

Cook, stirring, over medium heat until it comes to a simmer, then cook for another 10 to 15 minutes, or until the mixture resembles semi-thick custard. Stir in the cardamom powder to taste Pour the cream into serving bowls or glasses, cover, and chill in the refrigerator. Decorate with the nuts before serving.

### Caramelized rose almonds

These make a very special decoration. Dissolve 2 teaspoons of raw cane sugar with 2 teaspoons of water in a small saucepan, do not stir. Cook over gentle heat until the mixture turns a deep golden caramel. Take off the heat, add 12 blanched and split almonds and a pinch of dried edible rose petals, and stir to coat well. Using an oiled spoon, take them out and place on a greased plate and use as a garnish when they have hardened.

# Slightly Sticky Date Cakes

VATA
Ideal for vata

PITTA
Fine for pitta

**Makes 6 individual cakes; double the recipe for an 8-inch cake**

3¼ ounces fresh dates, pitted and chopped
1½ ounces prunes, pitted and chopped
⅔ cup water
½ tsp baking soda
3 tablespoons butter, at room temperature, plus extra for greasing
¼ cup raw brown sugar
1 egg
½ cup self-rising flour
½ teaspoon vanilla extract

**Jaggery walnut toffee sauce**
2½ ounces jaggery (dark unrefined sugar), grated or chopped or to taste
½ cup heavy cream
2 teaspoons butter
Handful of walnut halves
Pinch of salt

These cakes may seem indulgent, but the sugar comes mainly from the fruit and they have only a moderate amount of butter. I love them as they are or served with sweetened, preserved ginger-flecked cream. If you want to indulge, try the jaggery walnut toffee sauce. Jaggery is the healthiest sugar option as it is unrefined and full of minerals. This recipe is ideal for vata and will also not imbalance pitta, but is a little too rich for kapha.

Preheat the oven to 325°F. Butter 6 small dariole molds or muffin molds well.

Place the fruit and water in a pan and cook for 4 to 5 minutes, or until soft. Add the baking soda and blend to a fine puree. Whisk together the butter and sugar until creamy. Add the egg and whisk to mix. Stir in the puree, then follow with flour. Spoon evenly into each mold. Bake for 25 to 30 minutes, or until a toothpick comes out clean.

Melt the jaggery in a pan with a big splash of water. Add the cream, butter, nuts, and salt. Simmer until it is a light syrup. Pour over the cakes and serve.

# Simple Lentil and Coconut Dessert

VATA
Suits all doshas

PITTA
Suits all doshas

KAPHA
Can reduce cashew nuts and sugar; add raisins instead

**Makes 6 small portions**

Generous ⅔ cup yellow mung lentils
1 teaspoon ghee
⅓ cup cashew nuts
1 cup creamy coconut milk
1 tablespoon rice flour
3 to 3¼ ounces jaggery or 3 to 4 tablespoons raw cane sugar or to taste
¼ teaspoon green cardamom powder (grind the seeds of a green cardamom pod)
2 tablespoons dry unsweetened or flaked coconut

This is a great winter dessert for kapha as it is dairy-free and wheat-free. Lentil desserts are much loved in India and take many forms, all humble and simple which is the best way to eat according to Ayurveda. This is a typical no-frills dessert that is normally served in very small portions and is enough to satisfy a craving for sugar. Jaggery has different levels of sweetness and complexity, so add 3 ounces at first, then once cooked, taste and add more if necessary. This dessert is equally good for pitta and vata imbalances.

Dry roast the lentils in a skillet for 2 to 3 minutes, or until lightly roasted. Cool, wash well in water, and place in a saucepan. Add enough water to come 2 inches above the lentils and cook for 18 minutes, or until just soft. Drain off the water.

Meanwhile, heat the ghee in a small saucepan and lightly sauté the cashew nuts until just golden. Add the remaining ingredients and the drained lentils to the saucepan and cook over moderate heat for 6 to 8 minutes, or until the whole mixture comes together into an oatmeal consistency. Serve hot or warm, sprinkled with a little dry unsweetened or flaked coconut.

# Mount Everests

VATA
Great for vata

PITTA
Great for pitta

KAPHA
Eat only occasionally

I have always loved chestnuts. This dessert is obviously inspired by the well-known Mont Blanc dessert of meringue topped with chestnut puree, vermicelli, and heavy cream. My version is lightly spiced and served on fluffy pancakes instead of the meringues as I find them too sweet, thus requiring even more cream. This dessert is a real treat, but I do serve it in very small portions. It is neither too sweet nor too heavy. It is great for vata and pitta as it is nourishing and grounding but has no harsh or sour elements. As with most desserts, kapha should only eat as a treat.

**Makes 6 small Mount Everests**

Scant ⅓ cup water
3 teaspoons unrefined sugar
4¼ ounces unsweetened chestnut
   puree
¼-ounce piece preserved ginger,
   optional, I only add it if I have
   some to hand
½ teaspoon ground cinnamon
⅓ teaspoon vanilla extract
5 tablespoons heavy cream
1½ teaspoons vegetable oil
1 rounded tablespoon dry unsweetened
   coconut

**Egg-free pancake batter**
½ cup all-purpose flour (these are also
   perfect with white spelt flour)
¾ teaspoon baking powder
Pinch of salt
1 teaspoon unrefined sugar
⅓ cup milk
1 teaspoon butter, melted

Heat the water with the sugar in a small pan over moderate heat until the sugar dissolves and the water bubbles for 2 to 3 minutes, or until syrupy. Pour into a food processor and add the chestnut puree, ginger, cinnamon, and vanilla; blend to a fine puree. You can also do this by hand and finely grate the ginger in. Set aside.

To make the batter, sift the dry ingredients together into a bowl and make a well. Pour the milk slowly into the well, whisking all the time to avoid lumps and drawing down more flour from the sides of the well to combine. It should be a thick batter. Stir in the melted butter.

Whip the cream until it is firm enough to hold its shape once piped. To pipe, I use two small plastic sandwich bags, cutting the very tip of one of the corners of each bag to make a ⅛ inch opening.

Heat half the vegetable oil in a nonstick skillet. When hot, add 3 tablespoonfuls of the batter into the skillet, keeping the spoonfuls apart from each other in the skillet. The pancakes should be about 2½ to 2¾ inches in diameter and should retain a nice round shape. Lower the heat and cook for about 1 to 1½ minutes on each side, or until golden brown and cooked through. Repeat with the remaining batter.

Place a pancake on each serving plate. Spoon the chestnut puree into one of the bags or use a pastry bag fitted with the smallest tip. Pipe thin strands all over the pancake to recreate a bird's nest. Pipe the cream over the top in a similar way, using the second pastry bag. Sprinkle over the coconut and serve.

# Ginger and Soy Milk Chai

**Makes I large cup**

1½ cups water
¼ cup unsweetened soy (GMO-free) or rice milk
3 black peppercorns (pitta omit)
8 green cardamom pods, lightly bashed to open the husks
Small pinch of green fennel seeds
½-inch cinnamon shard
3 thin slices of ginger
I black tea bag (you can use green tea if you wish)
Honey, jaggery, raw cane sugar, or agave nectar, to taste

VATA Great for vata
PITTA Drink occasionally, omit the pepper
KAPHA Great for kapha

This tea is great for kapha and vata (who can also use cow's milk) as it is warming, especially in cold months. I have made my spiced Indian tea with soy milk for several years now, as I had decided to avoid dairy to see how it affected my well-being. Although I now drink some dairy, I prefer the taste of soy milk. Those with a pitta imbalance can also have an occasional cup.

Heat the water, milk, spices, and ginger in a medium saucepan. Once it comes to a boil, turn the heat down to low–moderate, and simmer for 20 minutes, or until the chai reduces down to about one large cupful. Be careful as the milk can easily rise and boil over, but a low temperature should prevent this.

Add the teabag and let it brew for I to 2 minutes, or until it is the strength you like. Strain into your cup and sweeten to taste.

# Honey and Spice Lassi

**Makes I glass**

scant ⅓ to generous ⅓ cup plain yogurt
⅔ to ¾ cup water
I to 2 pinches each of ground cinnamon, ground cardamom, and roasted ground cumin
Small pinch each of ground black pepper and ground ginger
6 large mint leaves
Honey to taste

VATA Great for vata
KAPHA Great for kapha

To roast cumin seeds, stir in a dry pan over medium heat for I minute, until aromatic, then grind to a powder. A great drink to aid digestion. Kapha: use ⅓ cup yogurt and ¾ cup water; vata: use generous ⅓ cup yogurt and ⅔ cup water.

Whisk all the ingredients together until slightly frothy. Stir in honey to taste and add more spices if you wish. Serve at room temperature.

# Sweet Mint Lassi

**Makes I glass**

Generous ⅓ cup plain yogurt
⅔ cup water
15 large mint leaves or to taste
1½ teaspoons raw cane sugar

VATA Aids digestion
PITTA Cooling for pitta
KAPHA Great in summer

This is a delicious, cooling drink for pitta. For vata, the fresh mint will help digestion. A great summer drink.

Blend all the ingredients together until the mint is finely shredded and the drink frothy. Serve.

# Pomegranate Juice with Fennel and Mint

**Makes I glass**

Generous ⅓ cup water
½ teaspoon fennel seeds
Generous ¾ cup pomegranate juice
3 mint leaves, shredded
Any natural, unrefined sugar to taste

VATA Great for vata
PITTA Especially good for pitta
KAPHA Great for kapha

Pomegranate juice is fantastic for all three doshas and is particularly good for pitta, although I recommend using the sweet variety and only when in season. Pomegranates cleanse the blood, aid digestion and are good for the heart and mind. Fennel seeds and mint add an extra dimension and are cooling on the body, which is perfect for pitta but work for all three doshas.

Heat the water and fennel seeds in a small saucepan until reduced to I to 2 tablespoons. Strain into the pomegranate juice and add the mint. Sweeten if you feel the need.

# Food Charts
## GRAINS

Whole grains are sweet, heavy, and nourishing. Vata should include lots of whole grains in their diet as should pitta, although they should avoid too much bran. Kapha should opt for small quantities of lighter, drying grains.

| Ingredient | Taste and properties | Vata | Pitta | Kapha |
|---|---|---|---|---|
| Barley | Sweet and astringent, cooling, light, diuretic | Exercise restraint | Good for you | Enjoy. Good for you |
| Basmati rice | Sweet, cooling, light, soft, smooth | Good for you. Brown better than white | Good for you | Exercise restraint |
| Bread | Sweet, salty, heavy, moist, soft | Exercise restraint | Exercise restraint | Avoid |
| Brown Rice | Sweet, heating, heavy | Enjoy | Exercise restraint | Exercise restraint |
| Buckwheat | Sweet and astringent, heating, light, and dry | Exercise restraint | Exercise restraint | Enjoy |
| Cornmeal | Sweet, heating, light, dry | Exercise restraint | Exercise restraint | Enjoy. Good for you |
| Dry crackers and cereals | Sweet, salty, dry | Avoid | Enjoy | Enjoy in moderation |
| Gram flour | Sweet, astringent, heavy | Exercise restraint | Enjoy | Enjoy |
| Millet | Sweet, heating, light, dry | Exercise restraint | Exercise restraint | Enjoy |
| Oats: dry and cooked | Sweet, heating, heavy | Cooked, good for you. Avoid dry | Both good for you | Exercise restraint, dry is better than cooked |
| Quinoa | Sweet, light, dry | Enjoy | Enjoy. Good for you | Enjoy |
| Rye | Sweet and astringent, heating, light, and dry | Exercise restraint | Exercise restraint | Good for you |
| Wheat (semolina, couscous, etc.) | Sweet, cooling, heavy, moist | Enjoy | Enjoy | Exercise restraint |
| White rice (polished) | Sweet, cooling, light, soft, smooth (not as nourishing as basmati) | Enjoy | Enjoy | Avoid |

## VEGETABLES

In Ayurveda, the aerial plant parts are thought to be stimulating, the roots grounding, barks and resins heating, and leaves and stems cooling. Vata should be careful of "windy" and raw vegetables—add some spices to aid digestion. Kapha should include lightly cooked vegetables in every meal. Pitta can enjoy raw or cooked vegetables. The vegetables from the nightshade family (tomatoes, eggplant, peppers, etc.) can be a little tricky for some. They can aggravate any joint problems and any allergies and if you have a very imbalanced pitta, their acidic content might worsen the problem.

| Ingredient | Taste and properties | Vata | Pitta | Kapha |
|---|---|---|---|---|
| Artichoke | Sweet, astringent | Enjoy | Good for you | Enjoy |
| Asparagus | Sweet, astringent, light, good for fertility | Enjoy | Good for you | Good for you |
| Avocado | Sweet, astringent, heavy, cooling | Good for you | Enjoy in moderation | Exercise restraint |
| Beet | Sweet, warming, heavy, smooth, relieves anemia | Enjoy | Enjoy | Enjoy |
| Broccoli | Sweet and astringent, cooling, rough, dry | Exercise restraint | Good for you | Good for you |
| Cabbage | Sweet, astringent, cooling, rough, dry | Exercise restraint (cook with spices) | Good for you | Good for you |
| Carrot | Sweet, astringent, heavy slightly warming | Enjoy | Enjoy | Enjoy |

| Ingredient | Taste and properties | Vata | Pitta | Kapha |
|---|---|---|---|---|
| Cauliflower | Sweet, astringent, cooling, rough, dry | Avoid | Good for you | Enjoy |
| Celery | Astringent, cooling, rough, dry, light | Exercise restraint | Good for you | Good for you |
| Corn | Sweet, astringent, heavy | Enjoy | Enjoy | Enjoy in moderation |
| Eggplant | Pungent, astringent, bitter, heating | Enjoy (see introduction). Cook with spices | Enjoy (see introduction) | Enjoy in moderation. Cook with spices |
| Garlic (cooked) | Pungent, heating, oily, smooth, heavy | Enjoy | Enjoy in moderation | Enjoy |
| Ginger | Pungent, heating, light, dry, rough, aids digestion, detoxifying | Enjoy | Enjoy in moderation | Good for you |
| Green beans | Sweet, astringent, heating | Enjoy | Good for you | Good for you |
| Lettuce (leafy) | Astringent, cooling, light, rough; excess can cause gas | Exercise restraint | Good for you | Enjoy in moderation and raw only in the summer |
| Okra | Sweet, astringent, cooling, rough, slimy | Enjoy | Enjoy | Exercise restraint |
| Onion (raw) | Pungent, heavy, heating | Avoid | Avoid | Enjoy in moderation |
| Onion (cooked) | Sweet, heating, heavy | Good for you | Enjoy in moderation | Enjoy |
| Mushrooms | Sweet, astringent, dry, damp, tamasic | Exercise restraint | Enjoy | Enjoy |
| Peas | Sweet, astringent, heavy | Enjoy | Enjoy | Enjoy |
| Peppers | Sweet, astringent, cold, sweet | Enjoy cooked and without skin | Enjoy (see introduction) | Enjoy, but remove skin |
| Potato | Sweet, astringent, cooling, dry, rough, heavy, avoid if you have arthritis | Exercise restraint; cook with spices | Enjoy in moderation | Enjoy in moderation |
| Radish | Pungent, astringent, heating, relieves gas, promotes digestion | Enjoy | Exercise restraint | Good for you |
| Spinach | Astringent, pungent, bitter, cooling, rough, dry | Enjoy in moderation | Enjoy in moderation | Good for you |
| Sprouts (cooked) | Mildly astringent, cooling, easy to digest when cooked | Enjoy in moderation | Enjoy | Enjoy |
| Tomatoes (cooked) (raw is bad for all doshas) | Sour, sweet, heating, heavy, see pages 56–57 | Enjoy in moderation (best eaten with spices) | Avoid | Exercise restraint (best eaten with spices) |
| Zucchini | Sweet, astringent, cooling, wet, light | Exercise restraint | Enjoy | Exercise restraint |

# FRUITS

Fruits are harmonizing, cleansing, and cooling, and are great in the mornings. Fresh fruit should not be eaten with other foods. Fruit is great for vata but should not form too much of the meal as it isn't grounding or nourishing enough for them. Vata should avoid all dried fruit unless well-soaked. Fresh and dried fruit and fresh juices are great for pitta, but avoid sour fruits. Kapha should eat fruit that is not too sweet (sweet fruit dampens agni) or too dense.

| Ingredient | Taste and properties | Vata | Pitta | Kapha |
|---|---|---|---|---|
| Apple | Sweet and astringent, cooling, light, rough | Exercise restraint with raw. Enjoy cooked | Good for you | Enjoy |
| Banana | Sweet and astringent, sour, cooling, smooth, heavy, can have laxative effect | Good for you | Exercise restraint | Avoid |
| Coconut | Sweet, cooling, oily, smooth, strengthening | Enjoy | Good for you | Exercise restraint |
| Dates (ripe) | Sweet, cooling, oily. Good for the blood. | Enjoy soaked. Good for you | Good for you | Turn away from. Exercise restraint |

| Ingredient | Taste and properties | Vata | Pitta | Kapha |
|---|---|---|---|---|
| Figs (ripe) | Sweet and astringent, cooling, heavy, nourishing, delays digestion | Good for you | Good for you | Exercise restraint |
| Grapes (purple) | Sweet, sour, and astringent, cooling, smooth, cleansing, strengthening, laxative | Good for you | Good for you | Exercise restraint |
| Grapefruit | Sour, sweet, heating, good for losing weight | Enjoy | Avoid | Exercise restraint |
| Lemons and limes | Sweet, sour, heating | Enjoy | Exercise restraint | Exercise restraint |
| Mango | Sweet, sour, heating | Enjoy | Exercise restraint | Exercise restraint |
| Melons | Sweet, cooling, heavy | Enjoy in moderation | Good for you | Exercise restraint |
| Oranges | Sweet and sour, heating, heavy, promote appetite but difficult to digest | Enjoy in moderation | Exercise restraint | Avoid |
| Peaches | Sweet, sour, astringent, heating, heavy | Enjoy | Exercise restraint | Enjoy in moderation |
| Pears | Sweet and astringent, cooling, light, rough, balance all doshas and hormones | Enjoy | Good for you | Enjoy |
| Plums (sweet) | Sweet, sour, astringent, heating, heavy | Enjoy | Exercise restraint | Exercise restraint |
| Pomegranate | Sweet, sour, and astringent, cooling, smooth, stimulates digestion. Good for the blood and detoxing | Enjoy | Good for you | Enjoy |

# DAIRY

Dairy is best when it is raw and taken from animals who are treated kindly. It nourishes all tissues, is calming and grounding, but can increase mucus and ama. Pitta should avoid all sour dairy products and yellow, hard, or very salty cheeses. Kapha should be wary of dairy products as they are heavy and cooling. Substitute with rice milk, almond milk, or soy milk. Dairy is good for vata (if you can properly digest them).

| Ingredient | Taste and properties | Vata | Pitta | Kapha |
|---|---|---|---|---|
| Butter, unsalted | Sweet, astringent, cooling, oily, smooth, promotes absorption | Good for you | Good for you | Avoid |
| Buttermilk | Sweet, sour, cooling. Made with half yogurt, half water and blended. Ideally, spice lightly and eat with meals to aid digestion | Enjoy | Exercise restraint | Enjoy in moderation |
| Cheese, white, soft | Sweet and sour, cooling, heavy, smooth | Enjoy | Enjoy in moderation | Exercise restraint (goat cheese is best) |
| Cottage cheese | Sweet, salty, sour, heating, smooth | Good for you | Good for you | Enjoy |
| Cow's milk (raw, see note in next column) | Sweet, cooling, heavy, oily, smooth. Easier to digest if boiled first, then cooled | Enjoy | Enjoy | Exercise restraint (goat milk better for you) |
| Cream | Sweet, cooling, heavy, oily, smooth | Enjoy in moderation | Enjoy in moderation | Turn away from |
| Eggs | Sweet, astringent, heating, smooth, heavy, oily | Exercise restraint | Enjoy | Enjoy |
| Goat's milk | Sweet and astringent, cooling, light. Relieves cough. Easier to digest than cow's milk. | Good for you | Good for you | Good for you |
| Rice milk | Sweet, light, unctuous | Enjoy | Enjoy (soy milk also good for you) | Enjoy in moderation (soy milk really good for you) |
| Sour cream | Sweet, sour, heavy, oily, smooth | Enjoy | Avoid | Avoid |
| Yogurt | Sour, astringent, heating, smooth, heavy, oily | Enjoy in moderation | Avoid | Avoid |

# MEATS AND FISH

Meat and fish are considered very nutritive but also difficult to digest, heating, and can breed toxins and create ama. For these reasons they are often avoided in the Ayurvedic diet. Having said that, weak Vata body types are advised to consume meat (often in the form of stews) as this is normally the best medicine for them. Meats and fish are heating so were not generally advised for pitta but some are better than others. Kapha are advised to cut down on both as well as they are quite heavy and hard to digest and kapha do really well on legumes and beans for protein. Lighter options are best.

| Ingredient | Taste and properties | Vata | Pitta | Kapha |
|---|---|---|---|---|
| Beef | Sweet, heating, very heavy, oily | Enjoy in moderation | Avoid | Avoid |
| Chicken/turkey | Sweet, astringent, heating, light | Good for you, opt for dark meat | Enjoy | Enjoy in moderation, stick to white meat |
| Freshwater fish (the best seafood option) | Sweet, heating, heavy, oily, smooth | Good for you | Enjoy in moderation (better than ocean fish) | Enjoy in moderation; opt for fish that is not oily |
| Lamb | Sweet, astringent, heating, heavy, oily, strengthening | Enjoy in moderation | Avoid | Avoid |
| Ocean fish | Sweet, salty, heavy, oily, smooth | Good for you | Enjoy in moderation, avoid shellfish | Enjoy in moderation, avoid shellfish |
| Pork | Sweet, heating, heavy, oily, promotes sweating | Avoid | Avoid | Avoid |

# OILS AND OTHER FATS

Oils maintain fat, nerve, and marrow tissue and are vital for the body, even when used externally for massage. Rancid oil increases ama so make sure your oil is not past its expiration date. In general, oil increases pitta. Kapha should take all oil in small quantities, even those that are good for them. Oils are good for vata. Avoid margarine.

| Ingredient | Taste and properties | Vata | Pitta | Kapha |
|---|---|---|---|---|
| Almond oil | Sweet, heating, slightly bitter | Good for you | Enjoy in moderation | Avoid |
| Butter, unsalted | Sweet, astringent, cooling, oily, smooth, promotes absorption | Good for you | Good for you | Avoid |
| Canola oil | Sweet, relatively light and drying | Enjoy in moderation | Enjoy | Great for you |
| Coconut oil | Sweet, cooling, relatively light, oily, smooth | Exercise restraint | Enjoy | Avoid |
| Corn oil | Sweet, astringent, heating, relatively light, oily, smooth | Exercise restraint | Exercise restraint | Enjoy in moderation |
| Flaxseed oil | Sweet, relatively light, heating | Enjoy | Enjoy in moderation | Enjoy in moderation |
| Ghee (clarified butter) | Sweet, cooling, light, oily, smooth, good for digestion and tissues; promotes longevity | Enjoy in moderation | Enjoy | Exercise restraint |
| Mustard oil | Pungent, heating, light, sharp, oily. Relieves arthritis and muscle sprain | Enjoy | Avoid | Enjoy in moderation |
| Olive oil | Sweet, cooling, heavy, oily, smooth, strengthening | Good for you | Enjoy in moderation | Exercise restraint |
| Peanut oil | Sweet, healing, oily, smooth | Enjoy in moderation | Avoid | Avoid |
| Safflower oil | Sweet, astringent, pungent, heating, relatively light, sharp, oily | Exercise restraint | Exercise restraint | Enjoy in moderation |
| Sesame oil | Sweet, bitter, heating, heavy, oily, smooth | Enjoy | Avoid | Exercise restraint |
| Sunflower oil | Sweet, cooling, oily, strengthening | Enjoy | Enjoy in moderation | Enjoy in moderation |

# SUGARS

White sugar will aggravate all the doshas and is often not properly absorbed so creates ama. Kapha should keep all sweeteners to a minimum; honey is the best choice for you.

| Ingredient | Taste and properties | Vata | Pitta | Kapha |
|---|---|---|---|---|
| Fruit sugar | Sweet, cooling, can cause ama | Enjoy | Enjoy | Avoid |
| Honey | Sweet, astringent, heating, dry, rough, heavy, cuts mucus | Enjoy | Exercise restraint | Enjoy |
| Jaggery | Sweet, heating, rejuvenative. Contains lots of minerals and vitamins | Good for you | Enjoy in moderation | Exercise restraint |
| Maple syrup | Sweet, bitter, cooling, smooth, unctuous | Good for you | Good for you | Avoid |
| Molasses | Sweet, heating, bitter, smooth. Good for iron deficiency | Good for you | Exercise restraint | Exercise restraint |
| Raw cane sugar | Sweet, cooling, heavy, smooth, oily, hard to digest | Good for you | Good for you | Avoid |

# BEANS

Beans and lentils can be drying and beans, in particular, can be a little windy. They are not great for vata as they increase their air content and overburden their digestive systems (small lentils are the best option). Beans and most lentils are good for pitta, who are able to digest them well. Most beans and lentils are good for kapha as they are full of nutrients, are astringent, and drying, and a better protein option over dairy and meats. Ideally cook with some spices. The best bean is the mung bean/lentil. See page 57 for cooking with beans.

| Ingredient | Taste and properties | Vata | Pitta | Kapha |
|---|---|---|---|---|
| Aduki | Sweet, astringent, rough, cooling | Exercise restraint | Enjoy | Enjoy |
| Black lentils | Sweet, strengthening, heavy, heating | Exercise restraint | Exercise restraint | Exercise restraint |
| Chickpeas | Sweet, astringent, cooling, heavy, dry, rough, windy | Exercise restraint (must be spiced or pureed like hummus) | Enjoy in moderation | Enjoy |
| Fava beans | Sweet, astringent, cooling | Avoid | Exercise restraint | Exercise restraint |
| Kidney beans (also navy and pinto) | Sweet, astringent, heating, dry, rough, heavy, laxative | Exercise restraint | Enjoy in moderation | Lightly increases/decreases |
| Mung beans | Sweet, astringent, cooling, light, soft, balances all doshas. Great to combat heat in the summer | Good for you | Good for you | Good for you |
| Red lentils | Sweet, astringent, heating, easy to digest | Enjoy | Enjoy in moderation | Good for you |
| Soy beans | Sweet, astringent, cooling, heavy, smooth, oily | Avoid | Enjoy | Good for you |
| Tofu | Sweet, astringent, cold | Enjoy in moderation (if you can digest) | Good for you | Enjoy |

# SPICES

Spices aid digestion and have healing properties. They are great for warming up kapha and vata. Pitta should stick to mild spices. Most supermarket spices have been irradiated which destroys their prana. If you have a health food store selling non-irradiated spices, give them a try.

| Ingredient | Taste and properties | Vata | Pitta | Kapha |
|---|---|---|---|---|
| Anise seed | Pungent, heating, light, aids digestion, detoxifying | Good for you | Exercise restraint | Enjoy |
| Asafetida | Pungent, heating, relieves gas | Good for you | Avoid | Good for you |
| Black pepper | Pungent, heating, light, dry, rough, aids digestion | Enjoy in moderation | Avoid | Good for you |
| Cardamom | Sweet, pungent, heating, aids digestion, good for heart and breath | Good for you | Enjoy in moderation | Good for you |
| Celery seed and ajowan seed | Pungent, heating, light, aids digestion | Good for you | Exercise restraint | Good for you |
| Chile powder | Pungent, heating, good for circulation and burning *ama* | Exercise restraint | Avoid | Enjoy in moderation |
| Cinnamon | Sweet, bitter, pungent, heating, relieves thirst | Good for you | Exercise restraint | Good for you |
| Cloves | Pungent, heating, aids digestion | Enjoy in moderation | Exercise restraint | Good for you |
| Coriander seed | Pungent, astringent, cooling, increases absorption | Good for you | Enjoy | Good for you |
| Cumin | Bitter, pungent, astringent, heating, light, oily, smooth, aids digestion | Good for you | Enjoy in moderation | Good for you |
| Dill | Sweet, astringent, heating, calming on the stomach | Good for you | Enjoy | Good for you |
| Fennel | Sweet, cooling, calming on the stomach, aids digestion | Good for you | Enjoy | Enjoy |
| Fenugreek (seed) | Bitter, astringent, heating, dry, good for arthritis, said to burn fat | Enjoy | Exercise restraint | Good for you |
| Mustard seed | Pungent, heating, oily, sharp, relieves muscular pain | Enjoy | Avoid | Good for you |
| Nutmeg | Sweet, pungent, astringent, good for digestion and the stomach | Enjoy | Enjoy in moderation | Good for you |
| Saffron | Sweet, pungent, bitter, astringent, cooling, smooth, good for all tissues, especially blood | Good for you | Good for you | Enjoy |
| Salt (general) | Salty, heating, heavy, rough, drying | Enjoy | Exercise restraint | Exercise restraint |
| Turmeric | Bitter, pungent, astringent, heating, aids digestion, helps relieve diabetes | Enjoy | Enjoy | Enjoy |

# Index

## Acknowledgments

I spoke to many doctors while researching and putting together this book. In particular, I would like to thank:

The doctors at the Leela Kempinski hotel in Kovalam, Kerala which is a beautiful vacation resort with an Ayurvedic health spa. They answered my most demanding and tedious questions, so thank you for your time.

Dr. Shyam, a reputable Ayurvedic doctor, of the Soft Touch Spa, in the Mall of Emirates, Dubai, for refining my knowledge on the subject.

A big, warm thank you to Rebecca Kriese for going through the manuscript, picking up on any errors, and for shedding light on areas of Ayurvedic confusion. Rebecca manages to seamlessly translate Ayurveda into modern life.

Thank you to Anne Furniss at Quadrille for encouraging me to write this book; I have wanted to do it for years but didn't know where to start. Also, thank you, thank you Lucy Gowans, Susie Theodorou, Gillian Haslam, and Lisa Linder for taking a serious subject and a complex book and making it so absolutely beautiful to look at and easy to read. Lastly, thank you Heather and Elly for your strong, unwavering support in matters both literary and practical.

I want also to recommend my favorite book on Ayurveda for those of you who want to learn more about this science, *Ayurvedic Healing* by David Frawley. It is the first book I turn to for Ayurvedic information. Find more information on David Frawley on www.vedanet.com.

There are many ways to find an Ayurvedic doctor, but here are some places to start.

National Ayurvedic Medical Association (US)
PO Box 23446
Albuquerque, NM 87192
Tel: +1800-669-8914, +1505-323-2838
www.ayurveda-nama.org

Ayurvedic Practitioners' Association (UK)
23 Green Ridge
Brighton BN1 5LT
www.apa.co.uk., info@apa.uk.com

Ayurvedic Medical Association UK
59 Dulverton Road
Selsdon, South Croydon
Surrey CR2 8PJ
Tel: 020 8657 6147

Dr.N.S.Moorthy@ayurvedic.demon.co.uk
British Association of Accredited Ayurvedic Practitioners (UK and EU)
31 Vicarage Road
London SW14 8RZ
Tel: 020 8392 2067
info@AyurvedaLondon.com

Australasian Ayurvedic Practitioners' Association
PO Box 481
Stones Corner, QLD 4120
Tel: (07) 38473428
www.ayurvedapractitionersaustralia.com

VEAT—(EU)
An der Falkenweise 9
85128 Nassenfels
Germany
veat@ayurveda-verband.eu
www.ayurveda-verband.eu